Charles Seale-Hayne Library
University of Plymouth
(01752) 588 588
LibraryandITenquiries@plymouth.ac.uk

ENVIRONMENTAL CHANGE: INDUSTRY, POWER AND POLICY

Environmental Change:
Industry, Power and Policy

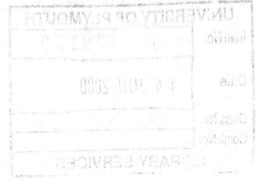

Edited by
MICHAEL TAYLOR

Avebury

Aldershot • Brookfield USA • Hong Kong • Singapore • Sydney

© M. Taylor 1995

Published by
Avebury
Ashgate Publishing Limited
Gower House
Croft Road
Aldershot
Hants GU11 3HR
England

Ashgate Publishing Company
Old Post Road
Brookfield
Vermont 05036
USA

British Library Cataloguing in Publication Data

Environmental Change: Industry, Power and
Policy. - (Organisation of Industrial
Space Series)
    I. Taylor, Michael   II. Series
    333.77

ISBN 1 85972 161 3 ✓

Library of Congress Catalog Card Number: 95-77723

Reprinted 1997

Printed and bound by Athenæum Press Ltd.,
Gateshead, Tyne & Wear.

Contents

v

PART II The state, policy and the environment

Figures and tables

List of contributors

Mark Bobe, Department of Geography, University of Portsmouth, United Kingdom

Sergio Conti, Dipartimento Interateneo Territorio, University of Turin, Italy

Egidio Dansero, Dipartimento Interateneo Territorio, University of Turin, Italy

David Gibbs, Department of Environmental and Geographical Sciences, Manchester Metropolitan University, Manchester, United Kingdom

Michael Healey, Department of Geography, Cheltenham and Gloucester College of Higher Education, Cheltenham, United Kingdom

Ray Hudson, Department of Geography and Centre for European Studies, University of Durham, United Kingdom

Simon Leonard, Department of Geography, University of Portsmouth, United Kingdom

Ooi Giok-Ling, Institute of Policy Studies, Singapore

R.K. Pandey, Department of Geography, Banaras Hindu University, Varanasi, India

M.B. Singh, Department of Geography, Banaras Hindu University, Varanasi, India

V. Singh, Department of Geography, Banaras Hindu University, Varanasi, India

Dietrich Soyez, Department of Geography, University of Cologne, Germany

Michael Taylor, Department of Geography, University of Portsmouth, United Kingdom

Paul M. Weaver, Department of Geography, University of Durham, United Kingdom

1 Linking economy, environment and policy

Michael Taylor

Introduction

This volume draws together contributions from a range of perspectives within economic geography on the place-specific and space-specific nature of the relationship between economic growth, transformation and change and environmental change. The separate contributions have very different starting points, but they all share a common goal. They seek to develop fuller understandings of the interconnectedness between, on the one hand, shifting patterns and structures of geographical industrialisation, and on the other hand, environmental-ecological change, coupled with attempts to ameliorate and control environmental damage, pollution and degradation through regulation, law and the force of policy.

In industrial and economic geography, as in industrial economics, industrial sociology and management studies, the object of analysis has been, for the most part, the organisation of production divorced from its very obvious environmental implications. With the widespread adoption of a political economy framework in human and economic geography, recent theoretical approaches have tended to emphasise relationships between capital and labour and, to a lesser extent, between capital and capital (see Peet and Thrift, 1989): between the owners of business and labour, and between businesses as they compete, co-operate, coerce and collude. These relationships have been cast in time and place-specific contexts to develop explanation and understanding of changing patterns of geographical industrialisation. However, in common with most other social sciences, nature and the physical environment has until very recently been excluded from this human geographic calculus. Just as Benton and Redclift (1994) have argued for the social sciences as a whole, economic geography has been preoccupied by the distinctiveness of human society, implicitly asserting that 'culture, meaning, consciousness and intentional agency [differentiate] the human from the animal' (p. 3). Economic geography has also shared economics' preoccupation with wealth creation, further avoiding the environmental clash by assuming that the environment is a free good. As a consequence, the nature-society dualism in economic geography represents a deep rift. The environment, by implication, is an unrestricted well of resources (no matter how they are socially constructed) and an unlimited (and therefore undamageable) repository for wastes. Thus, following O'Riordan's (1981, 1989) line of reasoning, economic geography, even in its newest political economy guise, is 'a *radical* or *manipulative* perspective [on society-nature relationships] in which human ingenuity and the spirit of competition dictate the terms of morality and conduct' (O'Riordan, 1989, p. 82). Nature is subordinate to humanity, and human actions are most properly interventionist (to produce a designed 'better' world) rather than being concerned with nurturing and stewardship. In short, it can be argued that much of economic geography starts from the implicit philosophical position that nature is unimportant and subordinate to wealth creation, a stance that contrasts strongly with the systems theory scientism of physical geography.

The challenge that confronts economic geography is, therefore, to more fully conceptualise the links between nature, economy and society and place them in a spatial context. Undoubtedly, as it is currently developing, such a conceptualisation is beginning to emerge within economic geography and the wider frame of human geography in general. Within that emerging conceptualisation a number of broad strands can be detected which in very general terms are concerned with:

- the social construction of the environment and environmental-ecological issues;
- the issue of structure versus individual agency;
- the question of the collective agency of business enterprises (as a distinctive form of purposive and negotiated agency);
- the undeniable physicality of the natural world and a continuing environmental imperative;
- the technological and technologists view of environmental change in terms of industrial ecology and industrial metabolism; and
- the state, policy and the environment: the environmental policy conundrum.

The strands of an environmentally aware economic geography

All of these strands are intertwined and interdependent and they are all integral to the warp and weft of a newly woven and environmentally sensitive and aware economic geography. They all contain significant dimensions of place and space that need to be incorporated into such a conceptualisation.

The social construction of the environment

The first important strand in the development of an environmentally aware economic geography is recognition of the fact that the concept of 'environment' is socially constructed. Different attitudes and approaches to the physical environment reflect the different ways people are incorporated into society. Culture acts as a screen, filter or distorting prism through which options for the use of the environment (including the recognition as well as the extraction of 'resources' and the dumping of 'wastes') are assessed and re-assessed through time and across space (Harrison and Burgess, 1994, drawing on Douglas, 1978 and 1982). The way we view landscape, countryside and the environment therefore 'reflects our social values and attitudes at any given time' (Redclift and Woodgate, 1994, p. 62), they are culturally contingent and nowhere more so than in the developed economies that have privileged scientism (Simmons, 1993). These views of 'nature' and 'the natural' vary from society to society and will evolve obviously as societies change. Indeed, for Norgaard (1994), society and environment will co-evolve 'as an interactive synthesis of natural and social mechanisms of change' (Redclift and Woodgate, 1994, p. 58). Society, especially in industrialised countries, will thus assume more and more control over 'natural' processes, intensifying pressures to further and more fully manage the environment in line with these evolving societal views.

Structure versus agency

This interpretation of the interconnectedness of society and environment immediately raises the issue of structure versus agency in the formulation of an environmentally sensitive conceptualisation of economic geography. Benton and Redclift (1994, p. 8) argue that the vast majority of individuals are locked into daily patterns of activity which they are unable to change even if they are aware that those actions are environmentally damaging. The power of individuals to make a difference in these circumstances is massively unevenly distributed, and this they argue is one of the most important insights that the social sciences can make to the environmental debate. This insight into the importance of structure has been provided with some clarity in human geography in the work of, for example, Blaikie (1985), Blaikie and Brookfield (1987) and Watts (1983). It is particularly clear in the developing country context that the social relations of production which enable surplus to be extracted from producers may force those producers to knowingly exploit and degrade their environmental assets out of desperation and simply

3

to survive (Emel and Peet, 1989).

These views on the significance of structure in determining interrelationships between society and environment feed directly into Harvey's (1993) structuralist critique in which it is argued forcefully (and at the same time well illustrated) that ecological projects are at the same time political-economic projects and vice versa. He shows very clearly 'the incredible political diversity to which environmental-ecological opinion is prone' (p. 20); that diversity ranges through 'authoritarianism', 'managerialism', 'pluralistic liberalism', 'conservatism', and 'moral community' ideals, to 'ecosocialism', 'ecofeminism' and 'decentralised communitarianism'.

But it can also be argued that individuals can make a difference in the way that society interfaces with the environment, and this is only too clear in the growth of environmental movements and the emergence of 'green' politics. In this view, people are goal oriented and able to unravel and explore their physical environments and to develop and build their own views of nature from within their own consciousness (Redclift and Woodgate, 1994, p. 54). Developing from this agency perspective is the view that the way individuals are incorporated into society perpetuates the way they see nature and society interacting and the way they judge the implications and consequences of those interactions (Harrison and Burgess, 1994). As outlined by Harrison and Burgess (1994), a typology of individuals' social involvement and their attitudes towards the environment has been elaborated in the work of Schwarz and Thompson (1990) and Douglas (1982). Douglas (1982) developed a typology of the manner in which individuals might be incorporated into society - a 'grid' and 'group' typology - reflecting the strength of the rules that regulate interpersonal behaviour (the *grid*) and the social relations of allegiance (the *group*). To this, Schwarz and Thompson (1990) added idealised conceptions of how nature responds to human actions through the metaphor of a ball moving in a landscape. A diagram of this combined typology is presented in Figure 1.1. Thus, the *individualist* sees nature as *benign*. The natural environment will recover no matter how it is exploited and, therefore, can be subordinated to wealth creation and the dictates of socially constructed markets. The *egalitarian* views nature as *ephemeral and fragile*. This is an ecocentric stance that favours consent, communalism and the minimisation of human impacts. The *hierarchist*, in contrast, is technocentric and swayed by the importance of 'expert knowledge' generated by a privileged science. In this view, nature is *tolerant to a point and thereafter perverse*. Finally, the *fatalist* sees life as a lottery and nature as *capricious*, random and not to be learned about through experience.

Very loosely, the elements of this typology can be aligned with O'Riordan's (1989) categories of environmental management and environmental politics developed in a European context. Individualism matches with intervention, technocentric managerialism and the politics of the free market, and may be a view held by as much as a quarter of Europe's population. The hierarchist is equally technocentric and an accommodationist in O'Riordan's terms. This perspective puts faith in experts so that society can accommodate the demands of the environment. It would appear to be a dominant view held by as much as two-thirds of society. In sharp contrast, ecocentric views are held by no

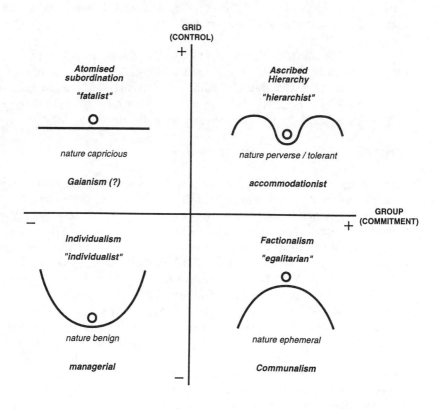

Figure 1.1 Cultural-political rationalities and 'nature'

Source: modified from Harrison and Burgess, 1994; incorporating Douglas, 1982; Schwarz and Thompson, 1990; O'Riordan, 1989

more than 10 per cent of the population. Egalitarianism equates directly with O'Riordan's communalism and radical socialism. However, Gianism sits uneasily with the notion of fatalism and it may simply be a sub-set of egalitarianism.

Exact correspondence between these sets of typologies is, however, not that important. What is important is that through O'Riordan's analysis a direct link can be made in the environmental context between structure and agency. It might be argued therefore that what is important in the development of an environmentally sensitive and aware economic geography is neither structure nor agency independent of one another, but the mutual dependence of structure and agency - Giddens (1979) structuration theory. This is very much the position adopted by Redclift and Woodgate (1994) in relation to sociology and the environment who have argued that:

> ... 'structuration' allows us to consider the environment as a structure which both enables and constrains human agency, while at the same time acknowledging that human agency may change the environment itself. In short, it enables us to take a much broader sociological view of the relationship between society and nature. (p. 54)

The collective agency of business enterprises

In dealing with agency in the context of an economic geographic perspective on environment-society interrelationships, it would also seem to be important to emphasise and highlight the collective agency of business enterprises and the networks of interdependence (both economic and social) within which they are embedded. It has been argued elsewhere that the business enterprise is a neglected analytical category (Dicken and Thrift, 1992; Taylor 1995). Clegg (1989, p. 188) has maintained that while all forms of agency are an achievement of control produced by discipline, the agency of organisations is a greater achievement because it involves 'the stabilization of power relations across an organizational field of action, and thus between many subjectivities' (p. 188). These temporarily stable coalitions are in fact the devices through which societies driven by wealth creation have had the greatest and most devastating impacts on the natural environment. They are the collective and simplified individualism of small firms and transnational corporations alike that can be employed to subsume personal and individual moralities that may not sit easily with the unconstrained pursuit of profit.

The essential physicality of the natural world

To this point, the strands that have been suggested as essential to be incorporated into an environmentally aware economic geography have been concerned with the social construction of the 'natural' environment and social reactions to environmental use and environmental issues. It is equally essential to stress the undeniable physicality of the natural world and the

6

continuing environmental imperatives of capacitated natural systems (such as the grand cycles) that are, so it is said, 'co-evolving' with systems of production and consumption that at the global level continue to expand exponentially. As Whatmore and Boucher (1993) have pointed out, 'while nature cannot be (re)produced outside social relations, neither is it reducible to them' (p. 167). In the rush to develop social perspectives on environmental issues, environmental change and environmental degradation, this vital point is all too easily forgotten. There is a continuing need to understand, measure and monitor the physical and chemical impacts of production and consumption on natural systems. One way to satisfy this need and to incorporate this strand is to incorporate into economic geography the very detailed thinking and understanding on the environmental degradation and pollution potentials of systems of industrial production that has been developed in the fields of 'industrial ecology' and 'industrial metabolism'. However, the incorporation of these concepts into an environmentally aware economic geography must recognise the substantial philosophical baggage that these concepts bring with them from their origins in positivist natural science coupled with neo-classical economics.

Industrial ecology and industrial metabolism

The concepts of industrial ecology and industrial metabolism have been outlined by Socolow (1994). Industrial ecology emphasises 'the industrial firm as an agent of change, and has located its analysis at the level of specific industries' (Socolow, 1994, p. xviii). The perspective is focused on firms, on relationships between industries and on opportunities for the wastes of one industry to become the useful inputs of other industries. As such industrial ecology is concerned with material and chemical transfers within and between industrial filieres. Industrial metabolism is more concerned with exploring system-wide transformations of materials associated with the long-term habitability of the planet, documenting pathways through which chemicals are released into the environment (through both production and consumption) and therefore documenting the routes to the toxification of the global environment (Socolow, 1994, p. xvii). The ideas draw on two research communities, the community of natural scientists studying global change, and the community of researchers concerned with technological and policy responses to environmental issues and forces moulding human activities (principally engineers and economists). The guiding principle of industrial metabolism is the notion of 'mass balance' - essentially a chemicals input-output accounting. Contentiously, stability and balance in structures of metabolism is seen to arise from price mechanisms which balance the supply of products and the demand for both products and labour (Ayres et al, 1988). Here is the most significant limitation of this approach, its roots in the market ideology of neo-classical economics. However, divorced from this ideology and separated from the scientific positivism of industrial ecology, these concepts have the potential to form vital stands in a reformulated and environmentally aware economic geography.

The state, policy and the environment

A final set of strands that needs to be incorporated into a reconceptualisation of economic geography concern the role of the state, regulation and policy in magnifying, ameliorating and facilitating the commercial use and exploitation of the natural environment. Working within the discipline and work regimes of a social-economic structure, individual agencies and collective agencies can be visualised as competing and jockeying for favour and support in order to gather around them allies and associates who are committed to their own, favoured modes of action and activity. In this way, key nodes of decision making will emerge in economic networks comprising individuals and business enterprises. These alliances, will also involve accepted norms of behaviour and business practice - Callon's (1986) 'obligatory passage points' created by rule fixing and by offering membership. Returning to the work of Douglas (1982) and Schwarz and Thompson (1990), the norms of behaviour associated with these obligatory passage points will also involve particular attitudes towards the sensitivity and susceptibility of the natural environment to commercial exploitation. Clearly, however, the state, governments and the frameworks policy and regulation they create are intimately involved in these processes of rule fixing and the sanctioning of membership. The state may represent no more than the dominant ideology in society (Johnston, 1989), for example, the interests of capital in a capitalist society as in Thatcherite Britain in the 1980s, but it may also be susceptible to the lobbying of interest groups, especially those concerned for the environment. The state is certainly involved, through the formulation and application of policy in shaping priorities for public intervention and expenditure - for example, prioritising expenditure on arms before expenditure on education, social security or the environment (O'Riordan, 1981).

This the role of the state and regulation in shaping approaches to the utilisation and exploitation of the natural environment is made more complicated, however, by the conflicting spatiality of both governments and environmental issues. Are environmental problems properly the province of local government, nation states or international, inter-governmental agencies? Can national governments pass all responsibility to local governments and yet keep to themselves 'reserve powers' over budgets for example. Can developed nations preach to developing nations not to exploit the natural environment in the way that they have? Do nation states or local governments

8

have the capacity or capability (or indeed the inclination) to control the 'industry flight' of transnational corporations and the 'export' of polluting activities?

The structure of the volume

The conceptualising project outlined above is large and involves the almost complete rethinking of economic geography. The chapters in this volume begin to explore and examine many of the conceptual strands that might contribute to a fuller and more environmentally aware and sensitive economic geography, and it is hoped that they will promote critical discussion of the agenda that has been mapped out.

Part I comprises five chapters that explore the environment-economy-place nexus from very different perspectives. Conti and Dansero question traditional, neo-classical approaches to environmental controversies and the current environmental debate, arguing instead for an ecological economics approach that rejects the false separation of people and nature. Hudson adopts a more structuralist stance and approaches environment-society interrelationships from the perspective of sustainability, arguing that ecological sustainability is not possible in the absence of economic and social sustainability. Taylor, Bobe and Leonard emphasise the role of business enterprises and collective agency in shaping economy-environment relationships. They contend that the conditions of network embeddedness and the dynamics of unequal power relationships (both within and between business enterprises) are vital processes moulding and modifying environment-economy contradictions. Weaver argues that to understand relationships between the environment and the economy it is necessary to account for industrial economic activities in material terms. To achieve this end he introduces product life cycle assessment and the notions of industrial ecology and eco-transition. Finally, Soyez adopts a networks and agency perspective to examine the geographical implications of environmental conflict triggered by resource use. Canadian hydopower schemes are used to focus attention on the politics of resistance, and conflicts between people, capital and the state, emphasising the spatiality of the relationships involved.

Part II comprises three chapters that focus on the role of the state in forming and modifying economy-environment interrelationships. Each chapter addresses this issue at a different scale. Ooi discusses the priority given to environmental issues within the policy frameworks of development oriented Singapore, and contrasts environmental issues in Singapore with the environmental degradation that is prevalent in many other rapidly developing East and Southeast Asian countries. Gibbs and Healey focus on the role of local government in formulating strategies for sustainable management of the local environment, using the UK situation to develop their arguments. They highlight the need for legislative and policy frameworks, and not just the mechanisms of the market, to stimulate and direct change. They show very clearly the conflict on environmental policy that can develop between different levels of government - local, national and supra-national. Singh, Pandey and Singh focus on environment-economy relationships in the context of a single Indian industrial estate - the Ram Nagar Industrial Estate in Uttar Pradesh. They demonstrate the conflict between the need for growth and the need for environmental protection, together with the problems of limited knowledge, lack of resolve in the enforcement of environmental controls and corruption.

References

Ayres, R., Norberg-Bohm, V. Prince, J., Stigliani, W. and Yanowitz, J. (1988), *Industrial Metabolism, the Environment and Applications of Materials-Balance Principles for Selected Chemicals*, RR-89-11, IIASA, Laxenburg, Austria.

Benton, T. and Redclift, M. (1994), 'Introduction', in Redclift, M. and Benton, T. (eds) *Social Theory and the Global Environment*, Routledge, London, pp. 1-27.

Blaikie, P. (1985), *The Political Economy of Soil Erosion in Developing Countries*, Longman, New York.

Blaikie, P. and Brookfield, H. (1987), *Land Degradation and Society*, Methuen, London.

Callon, M. (1986), 'Some elements of a sociology of translation: domestication of the scallops and the fishermen of St Brieuc Bay', in Law, J. (ed.) *Power, Action and Belief: A New Sociology of Knowledge?*, Routledge and Kegan Paul, London, pp. 196-233.

Clegg, S. (1989), *Frameworks of Power*, Sage, London.

Dicken, P. and Thrift, N. (1992), 'The organization of production and the production of organization: why business enterprises matter in the study of geographical industrialization', *Transactions of the Institute of British Geographers, New Series*, vol. 17, pp. 279-291.

Douglas, M. (1978), *Cultural Bias*, Royal Anthropological Institute, London Occasional Paper, no. 35.

Douglas, M. (ed.) (1982), *Essays in the Sociology of Perception*, Routledge and Kegan Paul, London.

Emel, J. and Peet, R. (1989), 'Resource management and natural hazards', in Peet, R. and Thrift, N. (eds) *New Models in Geography, Volume 1*, Unwin Hyman, London, pp. 49-76.

Giddens, A. (1979), *Central Problems in Social Theory*, Macmillan, London.

Harrison, C.M. and Burgess, J. (1994), 'Social constructions of nature: a case study of conflicts over the development of Rainham Marshes', *Transactions of the Institute of British Geographers, New Series*, vol. 19, no. 3, pp. 291-310.

Harvey, D. (1993), 'The nature of environment: the dialectics of social and environmental change', in Milibrand, R. and Panitch, L. (eds) *Socialist Register, 1993, Real Problems False Solutions*, Merlin Press, London, pp. 1-51.

Johnston, R.J. (1989), *Environmental Problems: Nature, Economy and State*, Belhaven Press, London.

Norgaard, R. (1994), *Progress Betrayed: The Demise of Development and a Coevolutionary Revisioning of the Future*, Routledge, London.

O'Riordan, T. (1981), *Environmentalism*, Pion, London.

O'Riordan, T. (1989), 'The challenge for environmentalism', in Peet, R. and Thrift, N. (eds) *New Models in Geography, Volume 1*, Unwin Hyman, London, pp. 77-102.

Peet, R. and Thrift, N. (1989), 'Political economy and human geography', in Peet, R. and Thrift, N, (eds) *New Models in Geography, Volume 1*, Unwin Hyman, London, pp. 3-29.

Redclift, M. and Woodgate, G. (1994), 'Sociology and the environment: discordant discourse?', in Redclift, M. and Benton, T. (eds) *Social Theory and the Global Environment*, Routledge, London, pp. 51-66.

Schwarz, M. and Thompson, M. (1990), *Divided We Stand: Redefining Politics, Technology and Social Choice*, Harvester Wheatsheaf, London.

Simmons, I.G. (1993), *Interpreting Nature: Cultural Constructions of the Environment*, Routledge, London.

Socolow, R. (1994), 'Preface', in Socolow, R., Andrews, C., Berhout, F. and Thomas, V. (eds) *Industrial Ecology and Global Change*, Cambridge University Press, Cambridge, pp. xiii-xx.

Taylor, M. (1995), 'The business enterprise, power and patterns of geographical industrialisation', in Conti, S., Malecki, E. and Oinas, P. (eds) *The Industrial Enterprise and Its Environment*, Avebury, Aldershot, pp. 99-122.

Watts, M. (1983), *Silent Violence: Food, Famine and Peasantry in Northern Nigeria*, University of California Press, Berkeley, CA.

Whatmore, S. and Boucher, S. (1993), 'Bargaining with nature: the discourse and practice of environmental planning gain', *Transactions of the Institute of British Geographers, New Series*, vol. 18, pp. 166-178.

Part I: Theoretical perspectives on environment and economy

The chapters in this part of the volume focus on different theoretical approaches to environment-economy interrelationships with different degrees of abstraction. Conti and Dansero focus on the environmental debate and controversies in the economic and territorial sciences and question traditional theoretical concepts. In particular, they advocate ecological economics as a way of understanding the relationships between economy and society because of its radical questioning of neo-classical and functionalist schemes of explanation. They see this approach as an holistic conceptualisation that does not admit the separation of society and environment, of people and nature. They discuss co-evolution, contextualisation and complexity, and the 'geographical challenge' of the concepts offered through the processes of 'territorialisation' and 'deterritorialisation'. 'Local' and 'global' are not seen as antagonistic, but as part of a single conceptual spiral. They argue that links between economy, society and environment are produced and reproduced locally and deployed more broadly, and that geography therefore becomes a science of places.

Hudson approaches environment economy relationships through the 'slippery' concept of sustainability, taking as a focus rapidly transforming capitalist economies. The concept of sustainability is constructed from the separate points of view of capital (and its need for profit), labour (and its need for employment) and the natural environment. From the discussion of these perspectives it is concluded that the interests of all three can not be satisfied simultaneously owing to fundamental incompatibilities. Thus, moves towards ecological sustainability must importantly be seen in terms of whether they are economically or socially sustainable - indeed, whether they are socially acceptable or politically legitimate.

Taylor, Bobe and Leonard approach environment-economy interrelationships from the perspective of business enterprises, stressing their constrained collective agency, unequal power relationships, their social embeddedness and their ability to affect the environment through their investment and reinvestment decisions. They employ the concept of 'industrial metabolism' to recognise route to toxification of the environment resulting from system wide transformations of materials. The conclusion is drawn from this analysis that business enterprises incorporated within dynamic networks of unequal power relationships may be incapable of acting to ameliorate mounting environmental problems, either locally or globally. Change will only be realised significantly altering the 'compulsory passage points' that guide the use and abuse of the environment in capitalist economies as they are currently configured.

Industrial metabolism is a theme taken up in the chapter by Weaver. Weaver addresses environment-economy relationships from the perspective of materials accounting, industrial metabolism and the study of eco-transition. It is argued that environmental damage arises from the materials throughput of industrial economies, and to change these flows will necessitate a massive eco-transition. Such a transition needs to be both efficient and effective, but they can also be used to create policies that may be economically unfair or that shift environmental problems from one place to another. These issues and concerns are examined and illustrated in the context of the European pulp and paper sector.

Soyez extends the agency and networks perspective of Taylor, Bobe and Leonard to examine the environmental conflicts associated with the James Bay hydropower projects in Quebec. He identifies the 'ecological shadows' cast over marginalised populations (often far removed from the places that 'benefit') by large scale industrial resource use in industrialised countries, and the resistance that is provoked. He maps the important transnational networks incorporating indigenous peoples, environmentalists and corporations that are integral to the protagonists' strategies and evaluates the repercussions from a industrial geographic point of view. Environmental conflict is seen to transform the sustainable development catch phrase 'think globally, act locally' into 'think locally, act globally'. It is concluded that it is only through a fuller appreciation of the network relationships of agencies of all types, and the 'spaces' they create, that the dynamics of industry-environment interactions can be understood.

14

2 The economy and the environment: Itineraries for the construction of a territorial approach

Sergio Conti and Egidio Dansero

Introduction

It would obviously be an illusion to try to draw conclusions in just a few pages about the environmental problem as it has developed in the social sciences in recent years. Among the many reasons for this are:

- the *conceptual syncretism* which characterises the various levels of knowledge of the environment (as exemplified by the number of definitions of a key concept such as 'sustainable development': some authors record 25 different definitions of the concept (Pearce et al., 1989), while the Bruntland report alone contains six (World Commission, 1987)); and
- the profound interdisciplinary debate on the environment which is almost inevitably partial and incomplete.

What is clear is that any attempt at theoretical organisation is inevitably limiting, often opening instead of closing fundamental questions of interpretation. The discussion that follows is necessarily partial and will focus on the environmental debate within the economic and territorial sciences and the underlying controversies. Economics has registered considerable progress in the development of environmental understanding through the progressive consolidation of an autonomous branch, environmental economics. Unfortunately, environmental economics remains excessively respectful of economic orthodoxy, and is marked by the vice of neo-classical reductionism. However, alongside environmental economics, a new current has emerged and is consolidating itself. This stems in part from the realisation that the environmental question has thrown down such challenges to economic science that are strong enough to force it profoundly to rethink its own philosophical and epistemological foundations, going back to concepts and approaches that had long been neglected by the neo-classical orthodoxy. This is ecological economics, certainly a minority current, but a well represented and expanding one, which attempts to free itself from the circumscribed framework of the discipline, not only in the social sciences, but above all looking to the natural sciences, and ecology in particular.

Deliberately, we shall not deal here with the evolution of the environmental question within geography. We recall only how a discipline such as geography finds itself in an anomalous position: traditionally seen within the disciplinary debate as the natural place for tackling the relations between people and nature, it has apparently lagged considerably in dealing systematically with the environmental question. It seems clear today how the diffusion of the functionalist paradigm in geography effectively blocked at the outset a 'rigorous' analysis of the relations between people and the environment, whose foundations were laid in the 1920s by Vidal de la Blanche and Lucien Febvre.

Geography has always run the risk of being superficial and generalist. However, this characteristic has been praised as a merit in the current debate on environmental problems. In fact, the possession of a weak and blurred epistemological background compared to apparently 'harder' disciplines in the field of the social sciences, such as economics, can paradoxically be advantageous. In reality, perhaps because of this 'weak' epistemological statute, geography's own assumptions and foundations are not challenged by the environmental question, in a phase when 'normalised' knowledge, based on specialisation and the separation between sciences, comes to grief when faced with its complexity. This helps to lay bare the myth of uniform knowledge and methodological and analytical simplification, and provides in contrast the founding criteria and concepts of a 'new' science that is being formed. As we shall see, these criteria are based in systems thought and emphasise the inseparability of economics, culture, ethics, environment and a 'refoundation' of the relations between natural sciences and social sciences.

Our proposal is thus to identify the contributions that recent epistemological reflection in the territorial sciences can offer to the construction of this project. To achieve this goal, the argument in the chapter will be developed in five steps. First, we develop a synthetic critique of the theoretical and methodological advances and limits of environmental economics. Second, we use this critique to outline the structure that supports ecological economics. Third, we place the new discipline within the framework of the broader, current, scientific debate on the philosophy and epistemology of scientific research. In particular, some fundamental contributions from the still hazy theory of complexity will be assessed, since these are receiving special attention in current geographical and territorial debate. Fourth, from work on complexity, we construct a framework of understanding which defines the challenge that ecological economics represents to the territorial disciplines. Finally, we attempt to locate this framework within the wider debate on the concept of local development.

From environmental economics to ecological economics

The rise in the early 1960s of environmental economics as a relatively autonomous field within economics is well documented. It was in that period that, in virtually all industrialised countries, the signs of irreversible damage to the environment became apparent, caused by the unbridled economic growth of the post-war years. The extent of this damage was echoed in the works of Barry Commoner (1971) and Rachel Carson (1962).

In economic thought, the environmental question had not, until then, affected the rational and analytical orthodoxy which had been the basis of neo-classical purity. The dominant approach - which Kenneth Boulding (1966) paraphrased as *frontier economics* - assumed the environment to be just another factor of production that was 'transformable' by a production system that sought virtually unlimited growth. In this sense, the economic orthodoxy possessed an evidently anti-ecological framework while, on an epistemological plane, an explicit separation existed between the economy and nature. This 'ethic' was seen in concrete terms in the functioning of economic mechanisms, with *growth* aimed at constantly going beyond the economic and technological *frontier* of existing capacity to transform and appropriate the resources of the environment (Westman, 1977; Pepper, 1984)[1]. The assumption implicit in this ethic - i.e., the generation of value through the production of scarcity - was manifestly contradictory. Nonetheless, its foundations were not significantly weakened by the spread of 'new' approaches to the environmental problem, beginning in the 1960s, which inspired the adoption of 'defensive' strategies and remedies to the problems created by the functioning of the development model.

The thesis of *environmental protection* and *resource management* (Colby, 1991) followed the innumerable cries of alarm which began to be raised with dramatic regularity and which still constitute the corner stones of the 'institutional' history of the environmental question in Western societies. Without any claim to providing an exhaustive list, it is worth recalling some of these cries of alarm: the publication in 1968 of the allegory *The Tragedy of the Commons* by Garret Hardin, which immediately found an echo in the Anglo-Saxon academic world; the publication of the famous *The Limits of Growth* by the Club of Rome (Meadows et al., 1972); the United Nations Stockholm Conference of 1972; the publication of the Bruntland Report (World Commission, 1987), which launched the concept of sustainable development at the international level, making it official. The more recent

United Nations Rio Conference (1992), which definitively consecrated the 'dogma' of sustainability, and where the major dilemmas and contradictions which characterise environmental policy at the end of the century were reflected is, in effect, the most recent step in a process in which an awareness has been reached of the global dimension of the environmental problem and concepts have been defined which now have paradigmatic value, for example *limitations, sustainability* and *development* (as distinct from growth).

In environmental economics, all this has been translated into styles of thought that were quickly channelled into the neo-classical line, accepting its fundamental principles and instruments, in particular the dogma of market equilibrium. Thus, while from the normative point of view the definition of 'optimum pollution levels' and the production of environmental regulations (standards, taxes, emission levels etc.) led to wider, theoretical acknowledgment of the environmental emergency, they served equally to legitimate viewing the environment as an *economic externality* (Kneese, 1977). Maintaining the criterion of cost as central, the introduction of the environmental dimension into the theoretical model did not ameliorate its methodological reductionism. In fact, assuming the environment as a potential and real cost factor - which thus needs to be produced and managed - sustainability itself is assumed as a *constraint* on the efficient functioning of the system (Pezzey, 1989). Maintaining the economic imperative unchanged, an 'economisation' of the natural, ecological environment is effectively produced (Colby, 1991, p. 204).

However, an important conceptual distinction in the analysis of positions on environmental problems and the concept of sustainable development can be drawn between technocentrism and ecocentrism (O'Riordan, 1989); a dualism that maintains considerable utility on a theoretical level (Adams, 1990). Environmental protection and resource management approaches lie along a continuum which separates the more markedly technocentric positions from explicitly eco- or biocentric theses (Worcester, 1985). They can be characterised by varying degrees of technocentrism, by their faith in the ability and usefulness of classical science, technology and conventional economic reasoning, and in their approach to the environment involving management, regulation and a 'rational utilisation' (Pepper, 1984).

In contrast, the nuances of *ecological economics* harbour stimuli, hypotheses and suggestions from the entire spectrum of the technocentrism-ecocentrism continuum, but with particular input from the ecocentric approach. However, ecocentrism, unlike technocentrism, is far from being a unitary approach, as it includes both romantic and transcendental interpretations, draws inspiration from certain oriental philosophies and is, in part, founded on the canons of the modern theory of ecological systems. Within it, in an attempt at great synthesis, it is, however, legitimate to identify a 'radically' ecological approach (*deep ecology*, according to the definition of Devall and Sessions,

18

1985) which presupposes an ideology of (economic) development based on alternative 'models' (decentralised, based on cultural diversity, not growth-oriented, and based on alternative technologies). Library shelves are packed with works which offer improbable imagery of development strategies 'in harmony with nature' (or the *anti-growth eco-topia)* to which a normative value is also attributed (self reliance, self centred development etc.) (Galtung, 1980; Nash, 1989; Trainer, 1990; Friedmann, 1992). Nevertheless, the social equity and the cultural concerns raised in the various schools of deep ecology represent fundamental questions for the construction of ecological economics.

One particularly interesting position within the ecocentric front is represented by the elaboration in terms of auto-poietic systems of a bio-physiological model of the earth system known as Gaia (Lovelock, 1979 and 1989). The Gaia hypothesis assumes the earth as a living, self-organising and self-regulating system: this is, as is well known, a theory which merges biology, atmospheric science and biochemistry, coining a new science, 'geo-physiology'. This hypothesis has triggered heated debate, and has aroused considerable controversy in environmental circles, as it has not yet been fully demonstrated that the Earth possesses auto-poietic capacities. However, from our particular point of view:

> ... it is not important whether the theory has been proven or not, and whether it can be. It is instead essential that the observations made so far to demonstrate or disprove it have in any case highlighted that local terrestrial and aquatic ecosystems, on which human pressure is increasing, possess effective self-regulating capacities, and behave as organisms, largely endowed with a high degree of complexity. (Vallega, 1994, p.15)

The Gaia hypothesis, as with the ecologistical approach outlined above, assumes the environment as the 'epicentre of sustainability' (in other words, sustainability refers only to natural ecosystems)[2]. However, because of its contrasting vision compared to that of neo-classical economics, and above all thanks to its theoretical and methodological structure of reference, it has played a significant role in the elaboration - certainly tormented and far from being concluded - of a 'new' co-evolutionary economy-nature paradigm (Norgaard, 1988)[3] which, as we shall see, explicitly assumes the self-organised systems approach.

Ecological economies as trans-disciplinary knowledge

The ecological economics hypothesis to which we wish to contribute obviously does not deny some of the conceptual contributions already discussed, although it avoids any assumption of linearity in its paradigmatic evolution. In the social and economic sciences, it is characterised by the radical questioning of neo-classical and functionalist schemes. Consequently, its logical and conceptual structure can only be understood when included in a broader reformulation of the scientific method. For these reasons, it can be contended that the environmental emergency has contributed decisively to the defeat of the mechanistic (and ontological) ideal of rational thought, thus representing a litmus test for assessing the limits of Western science.

We have seen how the Gaia hypothesis assumes the idea of a physical and environmental system capable of self-regulation. This conception is clearly antithetical to the dominant science, not only because it offers an opposing bio-centric (and ecocentric) vision, but above all because of its underlying method (based explicitly on systemic instruments), and on the idea of knowledge made up of complex relations and feedback between different theoretical fields (Bresso, 1993).

Some economists have already set out along this path, openly critical of the dominant neo-classical thesis, although their success remains negligible and still latent. A number are particularly noteworthy. William Knapp, starting out from Marshall's theory of costs, introduced the idea of:

> measuring the results of the private enterprise system with the help of a yardstick that transcends the market, and lays the foundation for a new formulation of economic analysis which includes the aspects of reality that numerous economists have been inclined to discard or neglect in that they are *not economic* (Knapp, 1963, p. 23)

The reformulation of the concept of *externality* in terms of the utility (or non-utility) function lead to the assumption that between actors there exist non-economic transactions. This was a radical theoretical break[4], as had been the introduction of the concept of *limit*. It was within this framework, as is well known, that the economic myth of unlimited growth and the indefinite possibility of taking resources from the environment was undermined (Boulding, 1966).

The most significant contribution to the reorganisation of economic thought 'freed' from the classical criteria of circularity, of the reversibility of processes and, thus, of the system's tendency towards equilibrium, came with the introduction of the concept of *irreversibility*. In this way, the principles of thermo-dynamics, and in particular the concept of entropy, were applied in economics (Georgescu-Roegen, 1971; Martinez-Allier, 1987). By introducing the idea of the non-separability and *circular inter-dependence* of society and environment, two fundamental results were attained. First, an

20

economic orthodoxy linked to an 'immutable' world[5] was irremediably snapped and, second, the bio-centric hypothesis of an ecosystem closed in on itself also faded. This ecosystem is now seen as incapable of self-regulation when faced with the individual and collective economic and social behaviour which is the basis of morphogenesis in the environmental system.

It is on these foundations that the proposal to construct a knowledge distinct from environmental economics takes shape and which, from the pages of *Ecological Economics* (Constanza, 1989), dictates its theoretical and conceptual bases:

1. the introduction of the concept of 'limit' is a turning point that cannot be separated from the introduction of the conceptual distinction between *growth* and *development* (Daly, 1990);

2. the assumption of ecological knowledge in economics brings the problem of the non-reducible *uncertainty* of economic and social activities and phenomena to the forefront; and

3. the inevitability of the relationship between economic and social thought and ecological knowledge is the basis for overcoming the division between natural and social sciences (or *sciences of the artificial*, using a neologism now a common term) which instead represents a constant in the traditional Scientific Method.

While not yet being able to count on a consolidated body of concepts and instruments, ecological economies puts itself forward as an interdisciplinary 'appeal'. It groups researchers and scholars from different culture backgrounds brought together by dissatisfaction with how their own disciplines tackle the environmental question. Within the economic and the territorial disciplines, it embraces those who are critical of a strictly neo-classical interpretation of ecological economics. It would seem appropriate, therefore, to ask ourselves, as human geographers stimulated by this theoretical project, about the contribution that we can offer to it. To achieve this, we have chosen to re-examine some of the principles that have matured in the framework of thought on 'complexity' and which are gradually being absorbed into the territorial disciplines.

Systems theory and the co-evolution of man and nature

The questioning of the mechanistic ideal of rational thought is not a challenge thrown down to science by a single discipline or group of disciplines. It is a challenge based above all on the construction of multi-dimensional

21

knowledge as the only strategy possible for understanding the chains which link the living world to the inanimate world. Traditional science expresses itself through a formalising, quantifying and reductionist culture, and is thus poor in ethical points of reference. The tradition of Western thought has effectively aimed, using the celebrated formulation of J.B. Perrin[6], at hiding the underlying structure which make phenomena intelligble, i.e., substituting a 'complicated visibility' with a 'simple invisibility'. The consequence has been the introduction of a linear logic of causality in the explanation of phenomena in natural sciences, as in the sciences of the artificial. The problem of the relations between sciences was not posed, as only one law - that of mechanics - was presumed to govern the universe at all levels. Classical and neo-classical economics (and it can be extended to geography of a neo-positivist and functionalist background) thus closes in on itself in the search for its own laws, without worrying about the universe that surrounds it, as the universe is governed by its own laws (Passet, 1992). This summarises the logic of the modern Scientific Method: the passage from the 'part' to the 'whole' implies no logical break, as the whole is the sum of the parts and the common interest is the conjunction of individual interests.

Faced with the *multi-dimensionality* of the relationship between people and nature, different cognitive strategies can act together in the construction of knowledge. In other words, knowledge is a scientific project characterised by inter-dependence and feedback between different logics and levels of organisation. *Complex thought*, in this light, expresses the need to react against abstraction and reductionism, which reduces nature to economics, and traces the relations between the economy, society and environment back to quantifiable (often monetary) variables (Le Moigne, 1992; Morin, 1977; Nicolis and Prigogine, 1986).

The recovery of certain *principles* at the centre of the upheaval in contemporary science can thus significantly open up hypotheses of interpretation and help us to get closer to a scheme of intelligibility. We shall limit ourselves to reviewing some of these principles. They are closely interlinked and have now assumed paradigmatic value.

The first principle is that of *creative destruction*. The thermo-dynamics of dissipative structures has been shown by Prigoigne and Stengers (1984) to be decisive for the comprehension of economic and social phenomena. It suggests, in particular, how evolution is subject to multiple dynamics, dependent on not entirely predictable *micro-events* which trigger bifurcations in the system, which tend to become more complex and to evolve according to uncertain and unpredictable trajectories. Evolution thus appears chaotic, an unceasing articulation of determinism and indeterminism, permanent creation and destruction of economic structures, socio-cultural values, and environmental equilibria. This explains the inseparable bond between *multi-dimensionality* and the introduction of a whole series of concepts of a second order such as chaos, disorder, noise and unpredictability. The image that emerges is far from that of reductionism or mechanistic causality.

It follows that *instability* and not equilibrium, is the normal situation for all systems (physical, biological or social), susceptible to constant morphogenesis under the effect of catastrophes or bifurcations (Thom, 1972). The *'Third State'* theory in physics, and above all the theory of *macro-evolution* in post-Darwinian biology (Laszlo, 1981), introduced instability as a 'normal' condition (and defined equilibrium as an extreme one), were decisive in resolving certain conceptual questions common to social sciences. In particular, they led to an understanding of *structure* not as an invariant in the evolution process, but as something itself susceptible to shifting complexity on contact with the external *environment*. Such shifting complexity can initiate changes that affect the system's capacity for *resilience*, which is understood as a measure of the system's capacity for adaptation to stimuli from outside environments.

The principle *of irreversibility* applied to the processes of evolution (as a consequence of successive bifurcations) leads to the replacement of the image of the system as a *banal machine* (where a given input produces a given output) with that of a *non-banal (self-referential and auto-poietic)*[7] *machine* (von Foester, 1981). The system, in other words, can give rise to an indefinite number of reactions, neither determined nor predictable. This assumption is determining, in that it contributes to 'keeping the General Systems Theory clear of risks of mechanistic visions' (Vallega, 1990, p.133). Evolution, in this light, cannot be determined analytically, but is unpredictable and dependent on history (i.e., on the structural transformations that have preceded it).

As the systems are *auto-poietic* (Maturana and Varela, 1980 and 1985; von Foester, 1981) and, thus, capable of defining their own limits with respect to the external environment, it follows that between the two systems - society and environment - close-knit communication is activated (a *consensual domain)* so that one system becomes the environment for the other. The system can thus be represented holistically in *bi-modular* terms: each of the modules - the physical world and the human world - is itself a system, representable as a non-banal, auto-poietic machine, and thus capable of transforming its own structure and redefining its limits[8]. The inevitable relation between the modules is the root of the 'levels of alteration and morphogenesis induced reciprocally in the environment and in society' (Vallega, 1990, p.133).

The principles of creative destruction, instability, irreversibility and auto-poiesis recalled here obviously do not exhaust the vast range of epistemological transition in progress in contemporary science. By rethinking scientific knowledge they appear capable, however, of giving full pertinence to the idea of the inseparability of the economy and the environment. More particularly, they allow the highlighting of some fundamental issues of a conceptual and theoretical nature:

- They replace the 'hierarchical' interpretation of the relationship between people and the environment (both the anthropocentric type and its opposite, the ecocentric kind) with an interpretation defined by a multitude of connections and which, as Bateson states (1979), assumes a 'critical relationship' between people and the environment. They are an expression of the dynamic character of natural and social equilibriums.

- They assume the dynamics of the people-nature relationship as a bi-modular systematic relationship, which is in antinomy to both mechanistic reductionism and even von Bertalanffi's vision of open systems, and indeed to the socio-centred interpretation (Luhmann, 1989) which reduces the environment to a factor of disturbance and 'echo' in society (Figure 2.1).

- The challenge of environmental knowledge cannot be simplified through traditional categories of analysis or through the juxtaposition of concepts taken from different disciplines. It involves not only problems of a philosophical nature, but also of an *epistemological* nature. In this light, the recourse to a *generalist* approach is not methodological reductionism, but the expression of interdisciplinary dialogue, which imposes itself when faced with a subject of multidimensional knowledge (Cameliau, 1994). It implies the limitation of each cognitive strategy (and paradigm) offering, in contrast, complementarity between different and non-reducible conceptual systems, each with its own theoretical and methodological baggage. In this sense, the role of disciplines such as geography is strengthened. For a long time they had seemed limited because they were not specialist disciplines.

- The re-affirmation of the ethical dimension in cognitive strategies cannot be isolated from the crisis of formalising and quantifying culture. The very debate on sustainable development has produced the resurgence of two great groups of ethical problems: the relationship between people and nature, and the relationship of rights and equality between people and between generations (what Laszlo (1981) defines as *universally human values*).

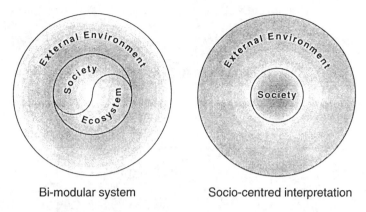

Bi-modular system   Socio-centred interpretation

Figure 2.1 Society and ecosystem: opposite visions
Source: Vallega (1990:185)

Images and instruments of a 'geographical challenge'

The range of concepts illustrated above can now be recomposed into *three levels of intelligibility* (or of knowledge, as Bateson (1979) says). They cannot be separated from each other, and neither can they be put into a hierarchy. On the contrary, they are part of a single, inseparable articulation (Figure 2.2).

At a first logical level, we can assume the *bio-sphere system* as an image of reference (Laszlo, 1981; Lovelock, 1979 and 1989). This is a 'complex organism' which has relations with the external environment (given by the sun as the source of heat). It has two modules, the socio-cultural system and the ecosystem. Thanks to the energy supplied by the sun, there is an articulated series of interacting feedbacks between these two systems which bind the evolutionary dynamic of society to that of the ecosystem. This is *a society-environment bi-modular system*, where both the subsystems are auto-poietic and, as non-banal machines, they assume behaviour that is neither determined nor predictable. The relations between the two modules (and the phenomena of change which follow) cannot be assumed without taking into account geographical scale. They involve simultaneously the global and the local scales, even if there are different *forms of contextualisation* on each scale. Think, for example, of a micro-process of air pollution (a micro event in the sense described above) which produces unpredictable repercussions on a vaster scale. In contrast, a process of change induced in the global eco-system (for example, variations in temperature at the global level) inevitably influence the local eco-systems (again in ways that cannot be determined *a priori*).

But, as we have seen, things are not so simple. The dynamic that directs

25

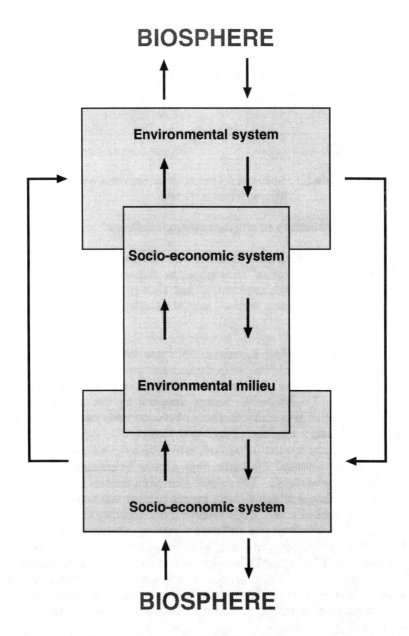

Figure 2.2 Contextualisation of the co-evolutive dynamic

the evolution of the system implies that each of its modules is open to the other, while each obeys its own logic of transformation. The perceived image is thus one of great complexity. The local contexualisation of a socio-economic phenomenon, for example, does not respond merely to the structural logics of its own system of reference (which do however act decisively). Complexity is created by the simultaneous activation of interdependencies in the environmental system. A micro economic event will thus act at the same time on the modification and evolution of the structure of the socio-economic system, on the specific social and environmental milieu[9], and on the global environmental system (the 'export of pollution, for example).

It would obviously be reductive, and ultimately mechanistic, to think that identical dynamics produces analogous global and local evolutionary effects. The specific diversities of individual milieus (environmental, economic, social, political etc.) create a world which has nothing in common with the Newtonian image of a repetitive universe. Environment, economy, society, culture and ethics, are all interdependent dimensions which define different forms of environmental interaction and, therefore, different paths to sustainability. Thus, the local dimension (in the sense of an individual and unrepeatable combination of social and ecological relations) asserts itself. The environmental question, in other words, cannot be isolated from the social (and therefore ethical and cultural) conditions in which it occurs.

Despite the unique and multidimensional character of territorialisation suggested here, a number of simple references allow this thesis to be illustrated. First, individual environmental milieus possess differentiated *carrying capacities* according to their own physical and chemical features and the historical pressures that act on them and affect their vulnerabilities. It is obvious, for example, that material and energy intensive industrialisation in the post-war period has irremediably compromised numerous environmental systems locally and globally.

Second, the organisation of production shows local specialisation, and production sectors show extreme variability in their consumption of natural resources and their release into the environment of externalities (either positive or negative). Furthermore, different forms of the organisation of production are territorially specific and have specific relations with their environmental milieus.

Third, the organisation of production is inseparable from the forms of *political and social organisation* (including environmental norms) which are an integral component of the people-nature dynamic. Environmental deterioration is not only a consequence of the industrial growth of the past two centuries. It is also as a structural expression of 'non-industrialisation'. In developing countries in particular, rural urban migration, demographic growth and the production of export crops are major threats to ecological systems (secondary salinity, deforestation, desertification etc.). They break down local social and environmental equilibria, with global implications. In developed countries, environmental problems usually receive most attention only in periods of economic expansion. Only rarely have political conditions been created that support environmental expenditure to support and relaunch the economy (Bresso and Raffestin, 1992), hampering the diffusion of industrial ecology, agri-ecology and ecological engineering (Sachs and Silk, 1988).

Fourth, the processes of *territorialisation-deterritorialisation* tend to occur locally. These processes define the historical and social identity of a system and, consequently, the relationships between society and environment. *Territory* is, itself, a product of the stratification of successive cycles of civilisation, in the course of which it absorbs 'the physical properties of the place' (Magnaghi, 1993). A process of deterritorialisation (of which there are many forms including abandonment, destruction of local culture, and standardising industrialisation) corresponds to a destructuring of the relationship between the physical environment and society.

By focusing on systems relationships, linear hypotheses of evolution and change can be seen to be inadequate. Contemporary knowledge thus appears *multidimensional*[10], in that it depends on complex (and non-repeatable) relationships between productive, social, historical and cultural components. These are the *constituent categories* of territory, expressing the multiplicity of the *ambits of identity*. A single and abstract mode of co-evolution between society (economy) and the environment does not exist. Instead, there is a multiplicity of critical relations (both of deterioration and sustainability) that cannot be separated holistically from the manifestation of global socio-economic and environmental processes.

Conclusions: towards territorial knowledge

In geography, and in the social sciences in general, the questioning of traditional theoretical concepts finds a logical recomposition in the concept of *local* (as in 'development'). This is a synthetic category upon which numerous paths of research on the rethinking of economic events and the interpretation of development converge. Despite a diversity of approaches (of Keynesian inspiration, and of the stadial and diffusive type), standard theoretical instruments found a unifying dimension in the functional paradigm which was analytically and normatively dominant in the early decades after the Second World War. Within this paradigm the general processes of development and change were assumed to dominate the specific economic, political, cultural and ecological environmental conditions of various local and regional situations. These local conditions were seen as obstacles to the 'diffusion of development'.

The 'crisis' of the functional paradigm is exacerbated by the reassertion of *holistic* approaches in the human sciences. This style of thought, which had been sidelined as metaphysical in the Cartesian method, tends towards a *globalistic* understanding of knowable phenomena and thus transcends analytical and reductionist decomposition of the phenomena themselves.

In very broad terms, the holistic approach has proceeded along three distinct paths. The first path is characterised by its approach to empiricism. Traditional means of analysis have been adapted to allow the new needs of theory to master the numerous 'deviations' of real processes from the old archetypes of reference (such as economies of scale and megapolitan growth). The theoretical syncretism which has come to the forefront in recent decades in the economic and territorial sciences can be explained by the inability of 'orthodox' models to understand the new and more complex forms of the articulations of development. The multiplication of concepts demonstrates this: 'bottom-up development' (Stöhr and Taylor, 1981), local technological potential (Ewers and Wettman, 1980), territorial development (Friedmann and Weaver, 1979), local development (Coffey and Polèse, 1985), production complexes (Storper and Walker, 1989; Walker, 1988). A *territorial logic* has established itself for the interpretation of socio-economic facts, in which the interdependencies and relations which are activated territorially (locally) between economic, social and institutional actors become the main players, while the advantages of agglomeration have come back strongly into the framework of interpretation.

The second path has developed from the epistemological reflection of a handful of unorthodox social scientists who, while having only a marginal effect on the dominant scientific institutions, have nonetheless had relatively profound impacts. The neo-Marshallian approach to the study of industrial districts is an eloquent expression of this impact. The debate is based on research on the social characteristics of territorialised economic systems, emphasising the heterogeneity of organisational forms. Industrial *atmosphere* (in some ways already present in Marshall's original conception) is seen to transcend pure economic phenomenon. Specific community phenomena are brought to the fore, and seen as the outcome of long-term historical and cultural processes, in contrast to the levelling tendencies of the modern global economy. This debate on the non-economic components of district environments has had significant theoretical effects. On the one hand, it has helped to undermine some of the 'certainties' on which conventional economic theory is based. On the other hand, it has led to the idea of the *intermediate entity* (between the actor and the overall system) capable of activating differentiated development routes and organisational models, and based on externalities that transcend market relations[11].

The third path is that which we have outlined here, based on a recomposition of scientific knowledge. It leads to the assertion of theoretical conceptions which are in open contrast with absolute and homologising styles of thought. As we have seen, its methodological force is significant, and it is based on a conception of science that does not admit separation between nature and people or between the natural and the social sciences. In this sense, the complexity of the local/global dynamic assumes its *full logical dimension*. As the foundations of a holistic approach, 'local' and 'global' are not antagonistic conditions but belong to a single conceptual spiral which precludes any idea of analytical fragmentation. It is locally (*territorially*) that the conditions and links between different but inseparable ambits (economic, political, socio-biological) are produced and reproduced for the deployment of broader economic, social and environmental processes.

In this light, geography once again becomes a science of places: not in a banal way, but as the expression of a multidimensional knowledge. Territorial understanding thus imposes itself as *generalist knowledge*, whose purpose is to discover structures and isomorphisms capable of telling 'true stories', fundamental invariants of the global dynamic of evolution.

Notes

1. In Marxist economic thought, the accent is put, in contrast, on distribution processes. However, this does not change the approach to the problem of the relationship between the economy and the environment significantly (Colby, 1991)

2. In the most radical criticism, the Gaia hypothesis has been defined in terms of a pre-rational utopia. In reality, the placing of the Gaia hypothesis among the ecocentric positions is debatable. It includes elements of both deep ecology and frontier economics, in that it is sometimes assumed as an alibi to justify any human intervention of the Earth. In addition, it considers the ecosystems' capacity for adaptation and includes the 'human factor' among those which contribute to the intrinsic processes of homeostasis of the planet (O'Riordan, 1989).

3. The term co-evolution refers to a process of feedback between two evolving systems. The co-evolutionist approach tries to establish a link between ecology and economic theory, considering economic development both as a process of adaption to a continuously changing environment and which is itself the origin of the change in the environment (Pearce and Turner, 1989). 'Norgaard makes a plea for a development model which does not reflect a unilinear view on progress, but one which encompasses a broad understanding of human/environment interaction. Thus, coevolution takes for granted a balance between economic development (all quantitative and qualitative changes in the economy that lead to a positive contribution to welfare) and ecological sustainability (all quantitative and qualitative environmental changes that serve to improve the quality of an ecosystem and hence have also a positive influence on welfare)' (Archibugi et al., 1989, p. 4).

4. It is on this basis, i.e. by distinguishing between private costs and social costs, that the economy of well being has developed (See Pigou, 1960; Baumol, 1965).

5. We are now far from the image evoked by Beckerman in 1974 in this exemplary passage, 'The problem of environmental pollution is nothing but a simple problem of the correction of a slight defect in the allocation of resources' (p. ?)

6. Later taken up by René Thom (1972).

31

7. The image of the non-banal machine is typical of systems that self-organise themselves. They possess two properties; self-referentiality and auto-poiesis. The former concerns the rules for its internal functioning and defines a circular process, on the basis of which every operation of the system refers to the system itself and is independent of the exterior. The latter, on the basis of which a system defines its own identity, envisages a circular process which reproduces the elements and relations between the elements (in other words, the structure) modifying them.

8. It would appear useful to specify the distinction between structure and organisation in the sense we use here. In the 'traditional' conception of open systems (following von Bertalanffi, 1968), the structure as a whole of components and relations is assumed as an invariant category, from which it is possible to identify and define the system. In contemporary systems thought, the role of invariant is assigned to the concept of organisation, which allows the identification of the system. The structure in this model, is susceptible to change in the course of its temporal evolution, as forms of manifestation of the system (Conti and Dematteis, 1995).

9. The concept of milieu is used here in the broad sense. It refers to located and specific sets of natural collective and socio-cultural conditions and resources, which appear in local development, as 'non-producible infrastructures'. It can be considered as the quality of place, deriving from long historical sedimentation. On the temporal scale of economic cycles they can consequently only be conserved and reproduced, or exploited and destroyed, but not produced de novo according to the needs of the moment, as occurs with normal infrastructures (Conti and Dematteis, 1995).

10. Just as the very concept of *sustainability* is multidimensional. It is not by chance that the Bruntland Report and Sachs himself recognised five dimensions of sustainability: social, economic, ecological, geographical and cultural (Sachs, 1989).

11. Here we have assumed the neo-Marshallian approach as emblematic of an upheaval which has also affected other disciplines. In economic sociology, for example, a heated debate has recently been opened that has brought to the fore concepts which go beyond the traditional boundaries for the discipline, such as 'structure of knowledge' and 'expert systems', as factors of integration between dynamically interacting actors (Block, 1990; Giddens, 1991).

References

Adams, W.M. (1990), *Green Development. Environment and Sustainability in the Third World,* Routledge, London.

Archibugi, F., Nijkamp, P. and Soeteman, F.J. (1989), 'The challenge of sustainable development', in F. Archibugi and P. Nijkamp (eds), *Economy and Ecology: Towards Sustainable Development,* Kluwer Academic Publisher, Dordrecht, pp. 1-14.

Bateson, G. (1979), *Mind and Nature. A Necessary Unity,* Dutton, New York.

Baumol, W.J. (1965), *Welfare Economics and the Theory of the State,* Bell and Sons, London.

Beckermann, W. (1974), *In Defence of Economic Growth,* J. Cape, London.

Block, F. (1990), *Post-industrial Possibilities,* University of California Press, Berkeley.

Boulding, K.E. (1966), 'The economics of the coming spaceship earth', in H. Jarret (ed.), *Environmental Quality in a Growing Economy,* John Hopkins University Press, Baltimore.

Bresso, M. (1993), *Per un'economia ecologica,* La Nuova Italia Scientifica, Roma.

Bresso, M. and Raffestin, C. (1992), 'Idee, valori e strumenti verso un sentiero di sviluppo sostenibile', *Sviluppo sostenibile,* IRRES, Perugia, 13-14 November.

Cameliau, C. (1994), 'Développement du développement durable ou blocages conceptuels?', *Revue Tiers Monde,* XXXV, 137, pp. 61-75.

Carson, R. (1962), *Silent Spring,* Houghton Mifflin, Boston, Mass.

Coffey, W.J. and Polèse, M. (1985), 'Local development: conceptual basis and policy implications', *Regional Studies.* vol. 19, no.2, pp. 85-95.

Colby, M.E. (1991), 'Environmental management in development: the evolution of paradigms', *Ecological Economics,* no. 3, pp. 193-213.

Commoner, B. (1971), *The Closing Circle,* Knopf, New York.

Constanza, R. (ed.) (1991), *Ecological Economics,* Columbia University Press, New York.

Conti, S. and Dematteis, G. (1995), 'Enterprise, systems and network dynamics: the challenge of complexity', in S. Conti, E.J. Malecki and P. Oinas (eds), *The Industrial Enterprise and Its Environment. Spatian perspectives,* Avebury, Aldershot.

Daly, H.E. (1990), *Towards a Measure of Sustainable Social Net National product,* Documenti Copamb, Centro Piani, Roma.

Devall, B. and session, G. (1985), *Deep Ecology: Living as if Nature Mattered,* Peregrine Smith Books, Salt Lake City.

Ewers, H.J. and Wettman, R.W. (1980), 'Innovation-oriented regional policy', *Regional Studies,* vol. 14, pp. 161-79.

Friedmann, J. (1992) *Empowerment. The Politics of alternative Development,* Basil Blackwell, Cambridge, Mass.

Friedmann, J. and Weaver, C. (1979), *Territory and Function. The Evolution of Regional Planning,* Arnold, London.

Galtung, J. (1980), 'Il faut manger pour vivre', *Cahiers de l'Institut Universitaire d'Etude du développement,* P.U.F., Paris.

Georgescu-Roegen, N. (1971), *The Entropy Law and the Economic Process,* Harvard University Press, Cambridge, Mass.

Giddens, A. (1991), *Modernity and Self-identity,* Policy Press, Cambridge.

Hardin, G. (1968), 'The tragedy of the commons', *Science,* vol. 162, pp.1243-8.

Knapp, W. (1963), Social *Costs of Business Enterprise,* Asia Publishing House, New York.

Kneese, A.V. (1977), *Economics and the Environment,* Penguin Books, New York.

Laszlo, E. (1981), *Le systémisme, nouvelle vision du monde. Pour une philosophie naturelle fondée sur les nouvelles tendences des sciences sociales,* Pergamon Press, Paris-New York.

Le Moigne, J.L. (1992), *La modélisation des systèmes complexes,*Dunot, Paris.

Lovelock, J. (1979), *GAIA: A New Look at Life on Earth,* Oxford University Press, New York.

Lovelock, J. (1989), *The ages of GAIA: a Biography of Our Living Earth,* Oxford University Press, Oxford.

Luhmann, N. (1989), *Ecological Communication,* Polity Press, Boston, Mass.

Magnaghi, A. (1993), *Per uno sviluppo locale sostenibile,* XIV Conferenza Italiana di Scienze Regionali, Bologina, 6-8 April (mimeo).

Martinez-Alier, J. (1987), *Ecological Economics: Energy, Environment and Society,* Basil Blackwell, Oxford.

Maturana, H. and Varela, F. (1980), *Autopoiesis and Cognition,* Reidel Publ., Dordrecht, Holland.

Maturana, H. and Varela, F. (1985), *The Tree of Knowledge,* New Science Library, Boston.

Meadows, D.H. et al., (1972), *The Limits to Growth,* Potomac Associates/University Books, New York.

Morin, E. (1977), *La méthode. I. La nature de la nature,* Seuil, Paris.

Nash, R.F. (1989), *The Right of nature. A History of Environmental Ethics,* University of Wisconsin Press, Madison.

Nicolis, G. and Prigogine, I. (1986), *An Evolutionary Theory of Economic Change,* Harvard University Press, Cambridge, Mass.

Norgaard, R.B. (1988), 'Sustainable development: a co-evolutionary view', *Futures,* vol. 20, no. 6, pp. 606-620.

O'Riordan, T. (1989), 'The challenge for environmentalism' in R. Peet and N. Thrift (eds), *New Models in Geography: The Political-economy Perspective. 1. Human Geography. Mathematical models,* Unwin Hyman Ltd, London, pp. 77-101.

Passet, R. (1992), 'La copitolage du développment économique et de lat biosphère', *Revue Tiers Monde,* vol. 33, no. 139, pp. 393-416.

Pearce, D. and Turner, R.K. (1989), *Economics of Natural Resources and the Environment,* Harvester and Wheatsheaf, Hemel Hempstead.

Pearce, D., Markandya, A. and Barbier, E. (1989), *Blueprint for a Green Economy,* Earthscan, London.

Pepper, D. (1984), *The Roots of Modern Environmentalism,* Croom Helm, London.

Pezzey, J. (1989), *Economic Analysis of Sustainable Growth and Sustainable Development,* Working Paper 15, Environment Department, World Bank, Washington DC.

Pigou, A.C. (1960), *Economia del benessere,* UTET, Torino (Italian ed.). Prigogine, I and Stengers, I. (1984), *Order Out of Chaos,* Bentam, New York.

Sachs, I. (1989), *Sustainable Development: From Normative Concept to Action,* Inter-American development Bank - XXX Annual Meeting Amsterdam, 3, pp. 23-89.

Sachs, I. and Silk, D. (1988), *The Food-energy Nexus Programme,* Final Report, United Nations University, Paris.

Stöhr, W. and Taylor, D.R. (eds) (1981), *Development from Above or from Below? The Dialectics of Regional Planning in Developing Countries,* J. Wiley, Chichester.

Storper, M. and Walker, R. (1989), *The Capitalist Imperative,* Basil Blackwell, Oxford.

Thom, R. (1972), *Stabilité structurelle et morphogénèse. Essai d'une théorie générale des modèles,* Benjamin, Paris.

Trainer, F.E. (1990), 'Environmental significance of development theory', *Ecological Economics,* no. 2, pp. 277-286.

Vallega, A. (1990), *Esistenza, società, ecosistema,* Mursia, Milano.

Vallega, A. (1994), *Geopolitica e sviluppo sostenibile. Il sistema mondo del seclo XXI,* Mursia, Milano.

von Bertalanffi, L. (1968), *General System Theory,* Braziller, New York.

von Foester, H. (1981), *Observing Systems,* Intersystems Publications, Seaside, Cal.

Walker, R. (1988), 'The geographical organisation of production systems', *Environment and Planning D. Society and Space,* vol. 6, no. 4, pp. 377-408.

Westman, W.E. (1977), How much are nature's services worth?, *Science,* vol. 177, pp. 960-3.

World Commission on Environment and Development (1987), *Our Common Future*, Oxford University Press, Oxford.

Worster, D. (1985), *Nature's Economy: A History of Ecological Ideas*, Cambridge University Press, Cambridge.

3 Towards sustainable industrial production: But in what sense sustainable?

Ray Hudson

Introduction

There seemed a time, extending for about twenty years after the second world war, in which, at least over much of the advanced capitalist world, more or less steady economic growth, profitable production and full employment were mutually compatible objectives. In this 'golden age' of modern capitalism, the era of a Fordist regime of intensive accumulation and mode of regulation, the productivity gains of mass production were validated by changing consumption norms and the growth of mass consumption. This equilibration of aggregate production and consumption was above all facilitated by state policies which tended towards mild income redistribution, encouraging growing private consumption, along with other state policies which involved growing public expenditure on the welfare state and led to rising levels of collective consumption. While mass production and consumption were unavoidably dependent upon and had perceptible impacts on the natural environment, this grounding of economy and society in nature was not generally seen as problematic. It did not seem that there were ecological limits to growth. For a while, then, it did indeed seem as if a new golden age of capitalism had dawned - at least in the First World if not the Third, as uneven development grew apace at global level as an integral part of the boom in the First World.

From the mid-1960s, however, all this began to change. Partly, this was because of the maturing contradictions within the Fordist model at a micro-scale within the factories. Workers became increasingly resistant to further intensification of the labour process and a proliferation of mind numbing deskilled and unskilled jobs within a deep Taylorist technical division of labour. As a result, the growth of labour productivity slowed and profitability fell. In due course, this led to a search for viable new micro-scale models of commodity production in all sectors of the economy. At a macro-scale, it became increasingly clear that the mode of regulation at national state level was becoming increasingly crisis prone. In part, this was because it became evident that state involvement did not abolish the crisis tendencies within the capitalist mode of production. In contrast, it transformed them and internalised them within the state. In due course, having simmered for a while, these crisis tendencies boiled over and dramatically appeared as crises of the state itself and its mode of crisis management (issues that are examined more fully below). No longer could national states seek to maintain full employment via Keynesian demand management policies, continue to expand collective consumption and public sector provision of services such as health and education, or increasingly, even set a floor level to living standards via the safety net of a welfare state.

Recognition of these limits to state capacities in turn led to a search for new macro-scale regulatory models that accepted and respected the state's limited powers to counter the forces of the market (forgetting, perhaps conveniently, that markets are social and political constructions, not natural structures shaped by forces beyond social control). One implication of this was that various 'post Fordist' regulatory experiments became characterised by much wider income differentials and a much greater degree of social inequality than had been the case in the immediately preceding period. If economic recovery did come about, it seemed certain that renewed growth would be achieved at the price of more unequal societies.

In addition, however, it increasingly became clear that the old Fordist model was remarkably blind to the ecological impacts of mass consumption and production. There is no doubt that industrial production had become a major cause of environmental pollution, both as a result of producing goods and services and then of consuming them. Indeed, it is the dissipative pollution generated by consumption that has a quantitatively much more significant effect on the natural environment than does production per se. Recognition of the links between mass production, mass consumption and environmental pollution, in principle at least, opened a window of opportunity to seek to combine economic recovery with greater environmental sensitivity in the organisation of production, circulation and the consumption of commodities. At the risk of some over-simplification, both prior to and during the Fordist era, the natural world was simply treated as a source of raw materials to be exploited with little if any thought about the impacts that this had on natural processes. In like manner, the natural environment was treated as a giant waste disposal site with infinite absorptive powers to cope with the pollutant effects of mass production and consumption. Innumerable noxious substances were carelessly discharged into the environment as unwanted by-products of production, through the transportation of goods and people, and via the emission of various pollutants into the environment in the course of consuming various commodities or through dumping them once their socially useful lives had come to an end. This was all done, however, without any deep knowledge of the environmental implications of producing and consuming in these ways. Once it became clear that nature in turn had an 'impact back' on human societies there was a growing ecological consciousness and 'green politics' of various hues from 'deep' to 'pale' emerged. It is certainly the case that strands of environmental thinking and advocacy had existed for a considerable period of time prior to the 1960s but these ecological concerns became more audible and visible in the latter part of that decade over much of the advanced capitalist world. Growing environmental consciousness was often tied to the causes of particular middle class interest groups, who enjoyed materially comfortable lifestyles and were seeking to preserve their own, often localised, environmental 'positional goods' (Newby, 1980). At the same time, however, some of them were becoming increasingly concerned with more general and global aspects of environmental conservation (see, for example, Nicholson, 1970). In addition, there was a more general growing concern with the 'limits to growth' as neo-Malthusian thinking grew in influence and there was, to a degree, coalescence around a common agenda of the need to protect the global environment (see, for example, *The Ecologist*, 1972). Despite the differences in immediate environmental concerns and in the depth of the shades of green, therefore, the emergent environmental groups all in various ways challenged the logic of Fordist mass production and mass consumption under the rubric of environmental conservation. By the 1980s, the focus of attention had switched much more to questions about environmentally 'sustainable' forms of production and consumption.

The meaning of 'sustainability' is by no means self-evident, however. Sustainability can be a very slippery concept actually to capture and pin down. Indeed, the concept itself requires problematising. Not least, this is because a key issue is to *whose* sustainability are we referring? To begin to answer this question, however, necessitates first conceptualising the organisation of the production process in general and of that within the social relations of capitalism in particular. Thus, capitalist production can be analysed as simultaneously a process of value creation, a labour process and a process of materials transformation. Examining the interactions of these varying aspects of the totality of the production process helps elucidate some of the problems of defining 'sustainability', both conceptually and practically. So in what follows I will introduce the concept of 'sustainability' and its various dimensions from the perspective of differing social interests who are involved in or otherwise experience the totality of this production process. Thus, 'sustainability' will be considered, for example, in terms of the social sustainability of the level and distribution of employment and of income, and from that of the ecological sustainability of the level and composition of output.

What is sustainable from the point of view of capital?

Our point of departure here is a recognition of the crisis of mass production and mass consumption that grew increasingly severe from the second half of the 1960s in the countries of the advanced capitalist world. There were certainly various national variations around the basic theme of the old 'Fordist' model of equilibrating mass production and mass consumption, with labour productivity gains going hand in hand with increased working class consumption norms. The fundamental point, however, is that this key macro-economic relationship became increasingly undermined as the internal contradictions of that regime of accumulation and mode of regulation became more and more exposed. The maturing crisis was reflected above all from the point of view of capital in a profound crisis of profitability.

In response to this, companies sought viable alternatives to the old mass production model: both alternatives to mass production and alternative forms *of* high volume (if not quite the old mass) production. The alternatives to mass production focused on small firms, skilled workers and flexible production. Such approaches placed considerable emphasis on networks and (allegedly) cooperative and non-confrontational relations between capital and labour and between companies linked in a mutually beneficial horizontal division of labour in a supportive regulatory environment. The *'rediscovery' of craft production* was, however, heavily influenced by the emergence of the 'Third Italy' and the rediscovery there of Marshallian industrial districts (Bagnasco, 1977). This led to a renewed emphasis upon the character of place as a - maybe *the* - key to industrial competitiveness.

Subsequently, there has been much debate about the extent, character and reproducibility of such industrial districts. There are, undoubtedly, clear limits to such an approach to production, in terms of products and markets (and also the number of jobs they will generate: see below); a fortiori, such forms of production are suited to niche market consumer goods from which the mass of consumers were, by definition, excluded as consumers. There is more than a suspicion that the creation of these new market niches was linked in part to the more regressive taxation policies and unequal income distributions that came to characterise most of the advanced capitalist world in the 1980s. Nevertheless, this apparent evidence of a successful local growth model led to a frenzied search for other successful new industrial spaces all over the world. Unfortunately,this was sometimes done in a rather uncritical fashion as places experiencing industrial growth based on diverse constitutive processes were heaped together into an increasingly meaningless category (for example, see Scott, 1988). Equally, against a background of high unemployment, it led many localities to seek to become 'pro-active' and to construct local economic development policies that would encourage the emergence of new industrial spaces in their territory (see Beynon and

Hudson, 1993). This place bound politics of local economic regeneration rapidly degenerated into a deeply divisive competition between localities in a global place market.

One consequence of the limits to the alternatives *to* mass production was, of necessity, the exploration of other approaches *of* mass - or perhaps more accurately high volume - production explored : *just-in-time* (Sayer, 1986); *lean production* which involves - or so its advocates maintain - an approach that '... can be applied in every industry across the globe' (Womack et al., 1990, p.6) with ' ... a profound effect on human society'; *flexible automation and dynamic flexibility* (Coriat, 1991; Veltz, 1991) which represent further attempts to combine the 'best' (from capital's point of view) of mass production and craft production. Thus, they sought to combine scale economies with economies of scope and greater consumer choice in response to greater market segmentation and differentiation. They therefore involve a combination of concepts from just-in-time - since they incorporate 'production to order' from a greater, but still relatively restricted, range of mass produced commodities. *Mass customisation* is a further attempt to combine the 'best' (from capital's point of view) of mass production and craft production, which takes the tendencies visible in just-in-time, lean production, dynamic flexibility and flexible automation a stage further. It seeks to combine the advantages of scale economies with batch production to create uniquely customised commodities i.e., mass customisation (Pine, 1992).

In fact, although presented as alternatives - not least by their messianic advocates in the major Business Schools - there is considerable overlap in what each of these approaches to production entails. Not least this is the case because they typically refer to the same sets of exemplar companies. For example, the 'Japanese roots' of lean production in Toyota's production strategies from the 1950s are reflected in many of the areas of similarity (if not identity) between it and just-in-time, though lean production certainly embraces more than does just-in-time.

Such 'new' approaches involve some significant changes in the organisation of production, *inter alia*:

- a restructuring of capital:labour and capital:capital relations;
- a restructuring of work and of the working class via new recruitment and retention strategies;
- an intensification of the labour process within workplaces;
- a reshaping of the social division of labour based more on selective relations of trust and cooperation between companies as a part of their competitive strategies (although it is clear that major asymmetries of power remain in relations between companies);
- the introduction of new systems of distribution as the implementation

41

of just-in-time concepts leads to the replacement of just-in-case stocks with inventories in motion. (with important ecological consequences as a result of increased movement and transport activity);

- a recasting of spatial divisions of labour away from the stereotypical geographies of Fordism (in a variety of ways, with differing local economic development implications: see Hudson, 1995) as companies seek to restore or enhance profitability in often volatile macro-economic conditions.

In brief, the emphasis is upon seeking to preserve the benefits of economies of scale while gaining those of economies of scope. This involves using existing and creating new forms of spatial differentiation as an integral part of this restructuring of production. It also encompasses introducing a greater element of product differentiation and consumer choice as the route to enhanced competitiveness and profits.

One point though is worth stressing. Insofar as these new approaches to production are alternative forms of mass production, (i.e., variations around the basic mass production theme - and I would argue strongly that they really are) then there are strict limits, in terms of the material and social requirements of commodity production, that will limit the range of industries and products in which they can be applied. Moreover, despite all the experimentation, there is considerable debate as to whether these approaches to production have revealed new ways of profitably organising production, especially on a longer term basis. And even if it can be argued that they have pointed to new ways of organising production at a micro-level, there seems little doubt that as yet no stable macro-level combination of regime of accumulation and mode of regulation has emerged as *the* successor to the mass production and mass consumption combination of Fordism. In this sense 'post Fordism' remains a clearly questionable proposition.

The social sustainability of the level and distribution of employment

The Fordist era was, at least for a while in much of the advanced capitalist world, characterised as one of 'full employment', albeit implicitly white adult male full employment. From the point of view of labour, the crisis of Fordism at macro-level has been experienced above all as one of high - and for many more or less permanent - unemployment. Equally, for those who succeed in finding wage work, there have been dramatic shifts in the sectoral pattern of employment, in the types of jobs on offer, in the terms and conditions on which they are offered in the labour market, and in the organisation of the labour process within workplaces. These changes, in turn, have been linked with an increasingly uneven income distribution and an expansion of poverty. There have been marked industrial and occupational variations in the incidence of unemployment, and associated primarily with this but also with an increasing number of poorly paid jobs, a growing polarisation between households with two wage earners and households with none (see Hudson and Williams, 1995). Growing poverty has been exacerbated by cuts in the welfare state as the restructuring of the labour market and of the state have reinforced one another.

The declining effective demand for labour is perhaps most clearly seen in relation to the new models of high volume industrial production. These employ far less living labour in the production process than did either Fordist mass production or small scale, batch and craft production. This can be most clearly seen in relation to lean production and its claim to be 'lean' because, *inter alia* compared to mass production, it only requires half the human effort in the factory. Certainly, unless aggregate demand is exploding, 'halving the human effort' can only mean a drastic reduction in the number of jobs available. Since a concern with economies of scale remains central in many industries, this almost certainly means less workplaces as well as less jobs. Unless the labour displaced in this way from such productive sectors is absorbed into other sectors of commodity production, the net result may well be a lower level of aggregate demand and greater uncertainty as to the prospects for corporate profitability. This in turn could well deter investment in newer and more environmentally sustainable production technologies. As a result, higher unemployment, lower output and threatened profitability could intertwine in a vicious downward spiral that locks production into environmentally unsustainable practices. It could even intensify these as companies seek 'spatial fixes' which would allow them temporarily to maintain profits at the price of yet more environmental pollution.

But if there are less jobs as a consequence of this shift to new high volume production methods, there are also strong claims that they are *better* jobs. There are claims from the supporters of the shift as to the beneficial re-emergence of multi-skilled workers, who are much more creatively involved in the process of production. Great stress is placed on teamwork, on reintegrating manual and mental labour, and on the 'empowerment' of production workers. Others dispute this. Critics argue that what is involved is not multi-skilling but multi-tasking, a very different attribute of a job, and the disempowerment of workers in new repressive regimes of control and surveillance of the labour process. As a result of the combination of these characteristics, in the new flexible high volume production methods, the line keeps running all the time. This does not mean that it *necessarily* runs at its maximum possible overall speed, nor necessarily at the maximum possible speed of each element of the labour process on the line. Indeed, the aim is not so much to maximise line speed as to minimise the number of workers needed for a given line speed (as dictated by the implementation of just-in-time principles of minimal or zero inventories). In this way the labour process is intensified, to the detriment of labour.

There are, then, increasing doubts as to whether the jobs on offer in the new production approaches are any better than those on the old mass production lines of earlier years. Indeed, there are definite suggestions that from the point of view of labour, these may involve greater intensification of work and greater stress than before. Not least, this is because teamworking involves a micro-scale regulation of the labour process in which workers discipline themselves and one another within and through the rhetoric of 'teamwork'. Moreover, since there are less jobs, there is enhanced competition for them and consequently firms can be extremely selective as to who they recruit and equally precise about the terms and conditions on which they will offer employment. The clear implication of this necessity for selectivity is that only a fraction of the available labour force will actually be employed.

Such changes in the amounts and forms of available wage labour are by no means confined to such innovatory manufacturing companies. On the contrary, in broad terms the last two decades over much of the advanced capitalist world have seen dramatic and generalised labour market changes. The processes driving these changes are above all corporate strategies of restructuring in the pursuit of profit and state strategies of restructuring in the face of threatening fiscal crises. The resultant labour market changes have been expressed in diverse ways. These include, a switch from manufacturing to service sector employment, shrinking public sector and expanding private sector employment, declining male and increasing female employment, declining full-time and growing part-time work, a decrease in secure 'jobs for life' and a growth in marginalised and precarious jobs. Such latter types of jobs are often in the informal sector or in or on the fringes of the black economy in 'flexible' and more deeply segmented labour markets as class, gender, ethnicity and age combine in complex and subtle ways.

Without doubt, however, the most pernicious effect of labour market restructuring has been the seemingly inexorable tendency to rising permanent (long-term) unemployment and under-employment, with all the social tensions and political pressures that growing poverty and widespread marginalisation brings. This is especially the case in the growing numbers of households with no wage earners, reliant on shrinking welfare state provision. The restructuring of production and labour markets has very visibly led to economic dislocation and the rupturing of stable reproducible social structures. The specificity of the interactions of general processes with the specific characteristics of particular places has generated different outcomes in different places (sometimes leading in turn to migratory pressures and questions to do with the regulation of migration, at various scales: Pugliese, 1991)

There is a real danger of a proportion of the population becoming permanently surplus to the requirements of capital: the old Marxist category of 'surplus population' may well be much more appropriate than that of 'unemployment' in describing this fraction of humanity. It would clearly seem that formerly valid concepts of 'full employment' - albeit often implicitly white male full employment - are no longer tenable. If, however, there is a continuing concern with issues of equity and social justice as a necessary condition for societies to remain civilised, democratic, reproducible and 'sustainable', then this suggests a pressing need to explore alternative ways of sharing out waged employment and of redefining citizens' rights to work.

Little more than a decade ago, the steel workers of Longwy marched through the Place de l'Opera in Paris demanding the right to 'live, learn and work in Longwy'. Now, so Lipietz (1992, p. 74) suggests, there is a need for a new social compromise in which the guarantee'... is not a "job", but 'the right to live and work in one's own "country"'. In other words, people must accept that there are no longer any 'jobs for life', a fortiori in one place for life, but that occupational and locational mobility must be accepted as the norm. The corollary of this is that the state must underpin such continuous change via sophisticated training programmes to preserve and enhance skills, especially transferable skills.

In itself, however, this will by no means necessarily solve the problem, for it implies that aggregate demand for labour is sufficiently high to absorb the available workforce. For this to happen, it will be necessary to share out the available waged work more equitably. This, in turn, will involve reductions in the working week and the growth of a 'socially useful third sector', providing work for around ten percent of the labour force (roughly speaking, the numbers unemployed at the start of the 1990s in the countries of the advanced capitalist world: Lipietz, 1992, p. 99). This reconceptualisation could also extend to incorporate new models of relations between waged employment and non-waged work - alternative 'bundles' of waged and non-wage work packaged together into household survival strategies (Mingione, 1985). This in turn problematises and forces a reconsideration of the links between production, reproduction and modes of regulation.

What then would be a socially sustainable distribution of work and employment? Put another way, what modes of regulation would be appropriate for different distributions of employment and income? These are key questions in the context of identifying socially sustainable models of production and forms of social organisation, locally (see Tickell and Peck, 1992), nationally and supranationally.

The ecological sustainability of the level and composition of output

Emphasising the importance of devising ecologically and environmentally sustainable forms of production has become increasingly popular in recent years, often in seemingly unlikely quarters. The World Bank (1994, p.42), for example, recently pointed out that '... achieving environmentally sustainable development is a major challenge of the 1990s'. This may well be correct, but part of the problem of evaluating competing claims as to what needs to be done is that there is by no means a consensus as to exactly what it means in practice. There are, for example, significant differences *within* the ecological movement between the various shades of 'green politics' as to what 'sustainable production' would entail. Implementation of some 'deep green' positions, would require significant reductions in material living standards and radical changes in the dominant social relations of production (see Goodin, 1992; Jacobs, 1991). There is no doubt that such changes would be powerfully contested. In contrast, rather 'paler green' perspectives are conceived much more in technicist terms within the current relations of production, essentially trading off economic against environmental objectives (see for example Pearce et al., 1989).

Perhaps the most quoted definition is that of the United Nations World Commission on the Environment and Development (1987, p.43) which defined sustainable development as meeting 'the needs of the present, without compromising the ability of future generations to meet their own needs'. Thus defined, sustainability encompasses the relations between the environment and the economy, and a commitment to equity, both intra-generationally, inter-generationally and spatially. It encompasses a vision of development that goes beyond quantitative growth in material outputs and incomes to include qualitative improvements in living and working conditions. In broad terms, it accepts rather than radically challenges the dominant logic of capitalist production.

There is no denying the impacts that human activities have had, and continue to have, on the environment, globally and locally. Of particular significance in the present context is the fact that industrial production, growth and transformation are the primary proximate causes of these impacts (see for example, Commission of the European Communities, 1992). In turn, environmental degradation and pollution has major impacts back on economic activities in a variety of ways. Yet as Taylor (1994) has cogently argued, the links between the dynamics of the economy and the dynamics of the environment have been only poorly and very partially drawn.

In order better to understand these links between the organisation of production and environmental change, we need to consider production as a process of material transformation. One way of doing so which allows some powerful insights into these relations between economy and environment are those of industrial ecology and industrial metabolism[1]. Industrial metabolism (Ayres et al., 1988; Ayres, 1989) is an approach which, at its simplest, involves constructing a balance sheet of the physical and chemical inputs to and outputs (both desired and undesired) from production (although this in itself is a far from simple task, with extremely demanding data requirements). It centres on the notion of mass balance - that is, that the sum total of a particular chemical within a production process remains constant as it passes from production, to consumption, to disposal, with human activity both in production and in consumption providing the stabilising controls. It therefore incorporates a conceptualisation of the production process as one of flows of physical matter, with the identification of pivotal points at which key chemical transformations occur and at which flows from the realm of social processes of production and consumption to that of the natural world take place. The crucial distinction between 'production pollution' and 'consumption pollution' (see above) is only implicit within the industrial metabolism literature but is nonetheless a crucial one to make, both analytically and in terms of exploring appropriate policy options (Taylor, 1994). There is considerable evidence to suggest that the latter is more pervasive and extensive than the former, not least because it has typically been less subject to restrictive regulation (see also below).

In brief, then, industrial metabolism describes the trajectory of flows of chemicals through an industrial economy and traces the discharge to and accumulation within the natural environment of the resultant pollutants. By tracing through the ecological impacts, in terms of inputs from and outputs to the natural environment, of particular methods and forms of organisation of production, the implications of possible choices of production technologies can be clarified. By tracing through the ecological impacts of varying combinations of the production and consumption of different levels and compositions of output, the macro-scale implications of micro-scale choices can be clarified. This would at least provide a base point from which to review the ecological implications of these varying social choices about the how and what of production. Moreover, it could in principle be extended to consider the where of production, for example, in terms of companies' attempts to find 'spatial fixes' for pollutant and environmentally noxious production.

A more precise identification of the ecologically damaging aspects of current methods of production and lifestyles and levels of consumption leads to a consideration of more ecologically sensitive approaches to production and consumption. One such approach is that which centres around notions of 'eco-restructuring' (see for example Weaver, 1993). In broad terms, this encapsulates the process of transforming modern capitalist industrial society from one characterised by high levels of use of virgin materials and fossil fuels, high levels of material consumption, and high emissions of wastes to one that is environmentally more benign. It could, therefore, be thought of as involving a transition to systems of 'clean production' (Allaert, 1994). The impetus for such changes once came from fears of exhausting non-renewable resources; of reaching and then breaching 'the limits to growth'. More recently it has been motivated by a recognition that there are limits to the capacity of the natural environment to absorb wastes. Consequently, there are limits to the robustness and reproducibility of natural processes as the variety and volume of pollutants rises.

One way forward is to examine the technical possibilities of and conditions for a greater degree of ecological closure in production and consumption (see for example Ayres et al., 1988; Weaver, 1994). There are, however, dangers of seeking 'technological fixes' in circumstances characterised by uncertainty and partial knowledge. One has only to think of examples such as the unanticipated environmental impacts of CFCs on stratospheric ozone, the substitution of diesel for petrol combustion engines leading to increased emissions of fine particulates, or the recycling of paper leading to increased chlorine emissions. Such cases are sharp and painful reminders of the unintended production of unwanted and harmful environmental impacts as a result of well-intentioned attempts to ameliorate other environmentally harmful effects. What, though, would be the geography of a more ecologically sustainable production system? How would moves towards ecological sustainability be conditioned by current patterns of uneven development and asymmetries of power relations within and between enterprises and societies, at varying spatial scales from the global to the local? These are important but as yet unanswered questions (see, however, Taylor, 1994)

Clearly, seeing production simply as a process of materials flows is at best a one dimensional perspective. One crucial limitation is that it abstracts production from its socio-spatial context. It therefore ignores the fact that production is a social process which has a definite geography, and which has manifold societal implications. The industrial metabolism approach is based on a biological analogy (Ayres, 1988) and, as such, at best incorporates a very limited conception of social process. In so far as it does incorporate a consideration of social process, it is in a very partial and emaciated form, with market prices seen as the only regulatory metabolic mechanism. The point that dissipative pollution as a result of consumption is a more generalised source of environmental pollution than that arising from production per se takes on added significance once one realises that the industrial metabolism approach places sole reliance upon the market rather than the state as a regulatory mechanism. Furthermore, reflecting its origins in neoclassical economics, it incorporates a simplistic and naturalistic view of markets and the mechanisms of price formation. It thus fails to give due weight to markets as socially constructed and regulated institutional forms. Moreover, it is clear that within capitalism a consideration of markets while ignoring property relations, the social relations of production and social class structures gives at best a very partial insight into the organisational dynamics of production. As a result, it also provides, at best, a partial view of the links between those and the dynamics of human induced environmental change.

At the same time, however, as a recognition of the socially constructed character of markets makes clear, it is important to avoid simplistic dualisms which posit the market and the state as dichotomous alternatives. Just as states are deeply implicated in the construction of markets, so too are they inextricably bound into the societies of which they are part. One implication of this is that state regulation does not necessarily offer a guaranteed and non-problematic resolution of the ecological problems generated by the industrial production system. Indeed, there is a considerable body of empirical evidence which supports such a conclusion and persuasive theoretical evidence that suggests that, with respect to a capitalist economy[2] this is unavoidably so as state involvement cannot abolish economic crisis tendencies inherent to such an economy. These are simply internalised within the operations of the state itself. As the analyses of proponents of the French regulationist approaches make clear (see Dunford, 1990), the best that (national) states can hope to achieve is to 'discover' modes of regulation that are temporarily appropriate to particular economic growth models, or regimes of accumulation. As a result, these will for a time allow the conditions necessary for successful production to be more or less non-problematically reproduced. The economic contradictions displaced into the structures and operations of the state itself in due course appear in fresh forms, for example as rationality, legitimation or fiscal crises of the state (for example, see Habermas, 1975; Offe, 1975; O'Connor, 1973). There is, therefore, no *a priori* reason to believe that state regulation will be any more successful in solving the even more complicated problems of environmental damage and ecological destruction that arise as a consequence of the character of production under capitalism.

In summary, there are evident grave dangers in examining possible changes to more ecologically sustainable forms of production without full consideration of either the social conditions that this presupposes or the implications of this for economic and social sustainability. It is vital to consider possible moves towards ecological sustainability in terms of *their* economic and social sustainability. It would be profoundly dangerous to ignore such issues. For example, would the level, composition and distribution of what is produced under an eco-restructuring programme be seen as socially acceptable and/or politically legitimate within the parameters of a democratic (as opposed to enforceable within those of a dictatorial) state form? If not, what would be the ecological implications of what would be socially and politically acceptable?

Conclusions

So where does this leave us? It is clear that there are no easy choices that will allow the interests of capital, of labour and of environmental survival to be simultaneously satisfied. Indeed, it is probably more realistic to recognise that there are fundamental incompatibilities between them but that at the same time they are interrelated rather than independent. It is worth recalling Harvey's point (1993, p. 22) that 'all ecological projects (and arguments) are simultaneously political-economic projects (and arguments) and vice versa. Ecological arguments are never socially neutral any more than socio-political arguments are ecologically neutral'. Indeed, he argues that the current preoccupation with concepts such as those of sustainable development represents a contemporary means by which capital is seeking the continuation of a particular dominant set of social relationships. This may well be an overly instrumental view, which underplays the significance of human agency in challenging the agenda of capital and its particular forms of industrial production. Equally, however, it is difficult to deny that the rhetoric of 'green products' and 'environmentally more friendly production processes' as a fresh source of profit for capital is an important input into the sustainability debate, seeking to reconcile capital's need for profits and labour's need for employment with a greater sensitivity to the natural environment. It is, however, difficult to see how such an attempted compromise can avoid the systemic and structural contradictions that beset all forms of capitalist production. This suggests that lasting solutions may well necessitate a close scrutiny of and radical changes in the dominant social relations of production rather than either tinkering with the problems at their margins via seeking various 'technological fixes' or seeking salvation via state regulation (supra-nationally or nationally) in an attempt to reconcile the irreconcilable. This may raise some very hard choices in balancing preservation of the undoubted benefits of generalised industrial production to the lifestyles of many people without violating the ecological conditions that make continuing human life possible.

Acknowledgements

This chapter was stimulated by discussions within the Human Dimensions of Global Change Working Group on Industrial Transformation at meetings in Fontainebleau, Laxenburg and Moscow. I am particularly grateful to Ashok Gadgil, Bill Moomaw and Paul Weaver for drawing my attention to literature on the environmental and ecological impacts of industrial production. I am equally grateful to Mike Taylor for discussions as to how to bring this together with the concerns of human geographers and social scientists in production as a social process that unavoidably involves spatially uneven development and for his helpful comments on the first draft of this chapter. Finally, Ian Simmons kindly and constructively commented on some very early ideas for this chapter and as a result steered me in directions of which I would otherwise have been unaware. He also commented on the penultimate version, and while the latest version is undoubtedly better as a result, he also raised some issues with which I have not even begun to deal. The usual disclaimers apply, however. I am also grateful to the HDGP programme for some financial support towards the costs of participating in these past meetings and trust that the process of discussion within the Industrial Transformations Working Group will continue to be an ongoing and fruitful one.

Notes

1. Although the concepts of industrial ecology and industrial metabolism are often used synonymously, it is useful to draw a distinction between them. Metabolism refers to the examination of the inputs of energy and materials into a specific facility, industry or sector, and the waste products - heat and materials - that are released from it. Ecology in this context refers to the total process from the raw material extraction, transportation, manufacture, use and disposal of products and the interaction of these with the natural processes of the biosphere.

2. There is an equally impressive (if that is the most appropriate term) volume of evidence that ecological devastation was at least as bad and frequently even worse under the political economy of state socialism. I am not aware of the sorts of theoretical arguments that have been advanced in relation to the capitalist state being developed in relation to the state capitalist, although it is quite likely that there were people who understood the ecological consequences but also the likely personal consequences (for example, via and enforced exploration of the Gulag Archipelago) of publicising this knowledge. There seems little doubt, however, that more general propositions about agents acting in circumstances of which they have only partial knowledge of the consequences of their actions (for example see Giddens, 1984) would equally apply in the circumstances of state socialism as they would in those of capitalism.

References

Allaert, G. (1994), 'Towards a sustainable scheldt region', in Voogd, H. (ed), *Issues in Environmental Planning*, Pion, London, pp. 131-44.

Ayres, R.U., Norberg-Bohm, V., Prince, J., Stigliani, W. and Yanowitz, J. (1988), *Industrial Metabolism, the Environment and Applications of Materials-Balance Principles for Selected Chemicals*, RR-89-11, IIASA, Laxenberg, Austria.

Ayres, R.U. (1989), 'Industrial metabolism and global change', *International Social Science Journal*, vol. 121, pp. 363-73.

Bagnasco, A. (1977), *Le Tre Italie: la problematica territoriate dello sviluppo*, Il Mulino, Bologna.

Beynon, H., and Hudson, R. (1993), 'Place and space in contemporary Europe: some lessons and reflections', *Antipode*, vol. 25, no. 3, pp. 177-90.

Commission of the European Communities (1992), *Towards Sustainability: a European Community Programme of Policy and Action in Relation to the Environment and Sustainable Development*, COM 92(23), Brussels.

Coriat, B. (1991), 'Technical flexibility and mass production : flexible specialisation and dynamic flexibility', in Benko, G., and Dunford, M. (eds), *Industrial Change and Regional Development : the Transformation of New Industrial Spaces*, Belhaven, London, pp. 134-58.

Dunford, M. (1990), 'Theories of regulation', *Environment and Planning D. Society and Space*, vol. 8, pp. 297-321.

Giddens, A. (1984), *The Constitution of Society*, Polity Press, Cambridge.

Goodin, R. (1992), *Green Political Theory*, Polity Press, Cambridge.

Habermas, J. (1975), *Legitimation Crisis*, Heinemann, London.

Harvey, D. (1993), 'The nature of the environment: the dialectics of social and environmental change', *Socialist Register, 1993, Real Problems False Situations*, Merlin Press, London, pp. 1-51.

Hudson, R. (1995), 'The end of mass production, the end of the mass collective worker and their respective geographies? Or more old wine in new bottles?', Paper presented to the Annual Conference of the Institute of British Geographers, Newcastle upon Tyne, 3-6 January.

Hudson, R. and Williams, A. (1995), *Divided Britain*, Second Edition, Wiley, Chichester.

Jacobs, M. (1991), *The Green Economy*, Pluto Press, London.

Lipietz, A. (1992), *Towards a New Economic Order: Postfordism, Ecology and Democracy*, Polity Press, Cambridge.

Mingione, E. (1985), 'Social reproduction and the labour force: the case of Southern Italy', in Redclift, N. and Mingione, E. (eds) *Beyond*

Employment: Household, Gender and Subsistence, Blackwell, Oxford, pp. 14-54.

Newby, H. (1980), *Green and pleasant land? Social change in rural England*, Penguin, London.

Nicholson, M. (1970), *The Environmental Revolution*, Pelican, London.

Offe, C. (1975), 'The theory of the capitalist state and the problem of policy formation', in Lindberg, L. N., Alford, R., Crouch, C. and Offe, C. (eds), *Stress and Contradiction in Modern Capitalism*, DC Heath, Farnborough, pp. 125-44.

O'Connor, J. (1973), *The Fiscal Crisis of the State*, St. Martins Press, New York.

Pearce, D., Markandya, A. and Barbier, E. (1989), *Blueprint for a Green Economy*, Earthscan, London.

Pine, J. (1992), *Mass Customization: the New Frontier in Business Competition,* Harvard Business School Press, Harvard MA.

Pugliese, E. (1991), 'Restructuring of the labour market and the role of Third World migrations in Europe', Paper presented to the Conference on Undefended Cities and Regions Facing the New European Order, Lemnos, 27 August to 1 September.

Sayer, A. (1986), 'New developments in manufacturing : the just-in-time system', *Capital and Class,* vol. 30, pp. 43-72.

Scott, A.J. (1988), *New Industrial Spaces*, Pion, London.

Taylor, M.J. (1994), 'Industrialisation, enterprise power and environmental change: an exploration of concepts', Paper presented to the IGU Commission on the Organisation of Industrial Space, Budapest, 16-20 August.

The Ecologist, (1972), *A Blueprint for Survival*, Penguin, London.

Tickell, A. and Peck, J. (1992), 'Accumulation, regulation and the geographies of post-Fordism : missing links in regulationist research', *Progress in Human Geography*, vol. 16, no. 2, pp. 190-218.

United Nations World Commission on the Environment and Development, (1987), *Our Common Future*, Oxford University Press, Oxford.

Veltz, P. (1991), 'New models of production organisation and trends in spatial development', in Benko, G., and Dunford, M. (eds), *Industrial Change and Regional Development : the Transformation of New Industrial Spaces*, Belhaven, London, pp. 193-204.

Weaver, P. M. (1993), 'Synergies of association: ecorestructuring, scale, and the industrial landscape', Paper presented to the Symposium on Ecorestructuring, United Nations University, Tokyo, 5-7 July.

Weaver, P. M. (1994), 'How life-cycle analysis and operational research methods could help clarify environmental policy: the case of fibre recycling in the pulp/paper sector', Paper presented to the IGU Commission on the Organisation of Industrial Space, Budapest, 16-20

August.

Womack, J. P. Jones, D.T., and Roos, D. (1990), *The Machine that Changed the World*, Rawson Associates, New York.

World Bank, (1994), *Annual Report 1994*, Washington DC.

4 The business enterprise, power networks and environmental change

Michael Taylor, Mark Bobe and Simon Leonard

Introduction

Industrial growth and industrial transformation, coupled with burgeoning mass consumption, have brought massive and measurable environmental change at all geographical scales, from the local to the global, with the result that ecological-environmental issues are of growing public concern. The local and regional impacts of the social economic processes of production and consumption have been readily apparent since at least the middle of the last century, but as local issues they have excited only local attention and have been either ignored or remedied by technical fixes. But now, many impacts are recognised as global and their effects are increasingly measurable, as in the case of the contributions of sulphur dioxide and carbon dioxide to global cooling and warming respectively (*The Economist*, 1995). Public concern about the environment is primarily centred (and, indeed, self-centred) on the implications for human activity of environmental 'health', environmental quality and environmental capacities (Harvey, 1993, p.2). 'Health' in this context refers to the condition of the ecosystems that support human activity. Issues of 'quality' pinpoint public concern over air, water and soil pollution, landscape damage and loss of bio-diversity. Concerns about 'capacity' highlight the continued ability of the natural environment both to provide natural resources and to absorb escalating quantities of waste.

In essence, therefore, environmental issues are conventionally viewed as external to the human condition; as though the maintenance of life is somehow disconnected from the business of making a living. Recognising environmental 'health', 'quality' and 'capacity' as quite separate from human activity imposes an implicit divide in these conventional views of environmental issues between, on the one hand, 'nature' and, on the other hand, 'culture' (Harvey, 1993). This same divide has been recognised in the social sciences generally by Redclift and Benton (1994) as an '... inherited nature/society dualism' that restricts the full appreciation of ecological processes in social scientific analyses.

Indeed, within geography, the links between the dynamics of economies and societies and the dynamics of the natural environment are just as poorly and partially drawn (Taylor, 1995, forthcoming). In the majority of studies of geographical industrialisation, the economy is postulated as a complex, socially determined mode of production driven by the labour process and divorced from the natural environment. Through omission, the environment is regarded as little more than a limitless source of materials and an equally limitless sink for wastes. The natural environment is, in effect, a public good of infinite capacity that can be used at no cost. However, for major groups of environmentalists (principally the ecocentric 'ecologists' rather than the technocentric environmental managers), the natural environment is a capacitated open system within which all human activity is embedded, and the use of which needs to be significantly constrained (see, for example, O'Riordan, 1981 and 1989).

Essentially, therefore, 'environment' and 'economy' are separately theorised in much of current geography. Even Johnston's (1989) attempt to theorise these links between environment, economy and society proved unsuccessful: in *Environmental Problems: Nature, Economy and State* the environment remained a capacitated open system quite separate from economy and society as a mode of production, and the state served only as a representative of the dominant ideology in society. Taylor (1995, forthcoming) has argued that the reason for the difficulty in gaining insights into the subtleties and details of the interrelationships between 'economy' and 'environment' is that the concept of 'mode of production' is too reified and obscures rather than illuminates these relationships: it does not translate to the realm of the concrete where our appreciation of local and global environmental problems is grounded.

In effect, using the reified notion of 'mode of production' to link the processes of economic and environmental change and transformation carries overtones of structural determinism in which the structuralists' patterned context locks out people and agency (Redclift and Benton, 1994). It is argued here that, without denying the importance of structure in certain contexts, it is only through a fuller understanding of agency, especially the collective agency of business enterprises and industrial organisations, that a fuller and more concrete appreciation of *economy-environment* interrelationships can be gained. It is within business enterprises, with their structures reflecting internal asymmetries of power, that the labour process operates. It is within these same business enterprises that capital is raised and accumulated, decisions are made on investment and production, and market manipulation takes place. Equally, it is at these enterprises and organisations that government policies and regulations on production, distribution, employment and environmental protection are targeted. In short, the business enterprise is the political crucible within which social, economic and environmental issues and forces meet and are played out in particular and specific spatial and temporal contexts.

In this chapter, an attempt is made to develop and elaborate this business enterprise approach to economy:environment interrelationships. The argument of the chapter is developed in four parts. First, from the economy perspective, the agency view of enterprise is examined to 're-embody' and make concrete environment:economy interrelationships. Second, from the environment perspective, the concept of 'industrial metabolism' is elaborated as a way of exploring materials transformations within systems of production and documenting the routes to toxification of local and global environments (Socolow, 1994). However, it too needs to be 're-embodied' within a business enterprise framework. Third, the business enterprise and industrial metabolism notions are incorporated into an enterprise power networks perspective to recognise explicitly:

- the unequal and asymmetric power relationships that bind productive organisations within capitalist economies;
- the impact of space and place in the shaping of these networks of competing, controlling and complementary organisations; and
- the environmental consequences that are implicit in those network topographies.

Finally, to introduce a dynamic and a temporal dimension into these enterprise network structures and their association with the use and abuse of the physical environment, the concept of circuits of power is introduced and elaborated. The aim is to clarify the links between industrial change and environmental change and, by examining 'economy' and 'environment' at the same level of abstraction and in the realm of the concrete (i.e., from the perspective of the business enterprise as a locus of decision making and unequal power), to clarify the dynamic interrelationships between them.

The business enterprise and collective agency

Within geography, analyses of economy and society that draw on either the well-established and largely atheoretic empiricist tradition, the precepts of an explicitly political economy framework, or the rapidly evolving constructs of social theory (especially regulation theory), have tended to have little direct concern for the impact of industrial growth and change on the condition of the natural environment. All have been preoccupied with developing fuller understandings of place-specific trajectories of economic change, principally in relation to the creation, destruction and reconstitution of jobs and work.

Geographical studies in the empiricist tradition have certainly focused on both business and work. Very loosely they have examined some aspects of *capital-capital* and *capital-labour* relationships, but in a very particular way. That way has been through the shoe-horning of business enterprises into gross typologies; large corporations, small firms, high technology producers, service industries and transnational corporations, for example (see the discussion in Taylor, 1995). In this same tradition, *capital-environment* and *labour-environment* relationships have been seen as quite separate and distinct one from the other; either as issues of landscape and land management or as problems that impinge on the quality of people's lives and their surroundings. In total, however, the insights gained from studies in the empiricist tradition of business enterprise dynamics, the changing nature of work and economic aspects of environmental issues do not add up to a consistent theoretical specification of the dynamic processes linking economy, society and environment. Indeed, they can only be characterised as, partial, inconsistent, serendipitous and unstructured. At best, they are small fragments of a greater, but unspecified, whole.

Geographical studies that have drawn on either a political economy framework or the constructs of social theory have been concerned, in contrast, to develop consistent though sometimes conflicting views of process (Peet and Thrift, 1989). In so doing, however, they have focused primarily on *capital-labour* relationships (Massey, 1984; Storper and Walker, 1983 and 1984; Walker, 1989) - a focus that continues through the flexible accumulation literature (Scott, 1988a, 1988b), locality studies (Cooke, 1989) and the regulationist perspective (Peck and Tickell, 1991; Dunford, 1995). *Capital-capital* relationships - the relationships between business enterprises - have been less adequately explored in these more theoretically informed aspects of economic geography. From a structuralist perspective, the business enterprise has been judged to be an irrelevant analytical category (Walker, 1989), while in some sections of the flexible accumulation literature both *capital-capital* and *capital-labour* relationships have been crudely reduced to the contractual straightjacket of Coasian transaction costs. However, within this broad political economy approach attention is increasingly being directed towards *capital-capital* relationships as part of an emerging networks perspective which recognises that individual businesses are bound into broad network structures of interaction, that inequality is the basis of network relationships and that those networks are centred on key nodes of decision making (Dicken and Thrift, 1992; Taylor, 1987).

Only relatively recently has attention been directed towards conceptualising *capital-environment* relationships (the interplay of 'culture' and 'nature') within geography's political economy perspective. Here, the outstanding contribution has been by Harvey (1993) who, working from a strongly structuralist perspective, argues forcefully and cogently that:

> ... all ecological projects (and arguments) are simultaneously political-economic projects (and arguments) and vice versa. Ecological arguments are never socially neutral any more than socio-political arguments are ecologically neutral. (p.25)

and more narrowly and cynically that:

> ... discussion of the environmental issue [might be] nothing more than a covert way of introducing particular social and political projects by raising the spectre of an ecological crisis or of legitimising solutions by appeal to the authority of nature-imposed necessity. (p.25)

To summarise, therefore, what characterises geography's current approach to the interrelationships between 'economy' and 'environment' in the context of industrial change and industrial transformation is, overwhelmingly, conceptual fracture. Ideas on the dynamic interaction of capital, labour, locality, the state and modes of social regulation are only partially and unevenly developed. 'Neither local nor global *capital-environment* and *labour-environment* relationships have been conceptualised in a way that would shed light on the impact of accelerating mass production and mass consumption on the capacitated global environment'. (Taylor, 1995, forthcoming)

It is proposed here that one potentially fruitful way to address this conceptual fracture is by moving from the realm of the abstract to the realm of the concrete, and by making the business enterprise the focus of analysis. This approach stresses the constrained collective agency of the business enterprise and makes central both the powerfulness and powerlessness of individual agents to 'make a difference'. This is important in the current debate on environmental issues because it shows very clearly:

> ... that the eminently rational appeals on the part of environmentalists for 'us' to change our attitudes, or lifestyles, ... are liable to be ineffective ... because the *power* to make a significant difference is immensely unevenly distributed. (Redclift and Benton, 1994, p.7 & p.8)

The argument to support the interpretation of organisation as a form of collective agency has been put strongly by Stewart Clegg (1989):

> ... organization [as] ... a form of collective agency ... is [not] ... a

61

second-rate form of agency compared with that of the problematic human subject. Where organization achieves agency it is an accomplishment, just as it is for the individual but more so, because it involves the stabilization of power relations across an organizational field of action, and thus between many subjectivities, rather than simply within one embodied locus of subjectivities. (p. 188)

Business enterprises and organisations do not slavishly follow the dictates and imperatives of capitalism. Their agency is a product of the people that own, manage and operate them, set against the cultures, economies and political structures within which they are embedded (Zukin and DiMaggio, 1990). Their use and abuse of the physical environment is not dictated by market pressures, processes and prices as has been suggested by economists in hypotheses on industry-flight and the creation of pollution havens (see the discussion in Leonard, 1988). Enterprise responses to environmental issues, constraints and potentialities are modified and shaped by three sets of contingencies:

- the processes of strategic management and strategic decision making that will reflect the perceptions and self images of key decision makers (Schoenberger, 1994) and the particular reserve powers that they exercise within any organisation or enterprise (Handy, 1994);
- the flows of information within and between both enterprises and decision makers and the condition of 'organisational slack' (Cyert and March, 1963); and
- the exercise of unequal power relations within and between business enterprises and the interplay of power and resistance within organisational structures and network relationships (Clegg and Dunkerley, 1982; Clegg, 1989; Barbalet, 1985).

Simultaneously, these contingent processes operate within time-specific and place-specific frameworks of social and cultural constraints and regimes of regulation (Clegg, 1990; Dunford, 1995). For Christopherson (1993), these frameworks of regulation can be 'system forming' or 'system guiding', and in terms of collective agency they increase the diversity of response, reaction and decision making among business organisations and enterprises. Indeed, on environmental issues, what may be appropriate and sanctioned commercial practice in one culture might be completely unacceptable in another.

However, the internationalisation and globalisation of economic activity further complicates the diversity of potential collective agency. As corporations have become larger and geographically more extensive they have begun to transcend the social, cultural and political systems and systems of regulation within which they are embedded. It would seem quite possible under these circumstances for actions, behaviour and responses appropriate in one context to be internationalised to less appropriate contexts. In other words, in the context of collective agency it is possible for the local to confound the global. This diversity of business enterprise agency denies the uniformity of action and behaviour that a strongly structuralist approach would suggest (see Walker, 1989). It is suggested here that only in the context of the constrained collective agency of business organisations and enterprises advocated by Clegg can the processes of industrial transformation and industrial change be linked conceptually with the processes of environmental transformation and environmental change.

However, understanding of the processes of environmental change still tends to be divorced from the dynamic context of the collective agencies that impact upon them. The processes of environmental change at the global and local scales tend to be reified and disengaged from the business enterprises and organisations that initiate, intensify and drive them. For economists in particular, 'economy' is essentially a price fixing mechanism, and dealing with the environmental consequences of production and consumption is simply a problem of establishing appropriate price signals (see the papers in Socolow et al., 1994 and the incisive critique in Jacobs, 1994). A first step in developing a business enterprise and agency view of environmental change and transformation is offered by the concept of *industrial metabolism*, an approach limited by its inadequate treatment of agency but made appealing by its exploration of system wide transformations of materials and its concern to document the routes to toxification of the global environment (Socolow, 1994a, p. xvii). The usefulness of this concept will be explored in the next section.

Industrial metabolism

Industrial metabolism is a technological and technologists view of environmental change which is capable of extension to incorporate the agency role of business enterprises while at the same time charting the interchange of materials and pollutants between 'economy' and 'environment'. It is an holistic methodology, a balance sheet approach, in which the movement of chemicals through industrial systems is tracked to identify points of production and consumption where chemicals are transformed and where they pass from the economy to the environment. Through this methodology, the release of chemical pollutants from production processes ('production pollution') and final consumption ('consumption pollution' associated with the release of substances through dissipative use and as post-consumption waste) is seen as part of a mass balance such that the sum total of chemicals moving through a system remains constant (Clark, 1988; Ayres et al., 1989; Stigliani and Jaffe, 1993; Guelorget et al., 1993).

When viewed in this way, industrial metabolism is very much a chemicals input/output approach in which the spatial scale of analysis is seen most appropriately as the river basin. Although the approach is applicable at a wide variety of spatial scales - from the global to the local - the river basin has been identified as the preferred unit of spatial analysis since it is contended that this is the scale at which transboundary fluxes are minimised and 'economic' space most nearly coincides with the 'environmental' space into which pollutants are discharged and accumulate. Adding a temporal dimension to the spatial dimension of industrial metabolism then leads directly to the notion of 'chemical time bombs', for as pollutants build to critical levels in particular localities they hold the potential to trigger local environmental disasters (Stigliani, 1991; Hesterberg et al., 1992).

Metabolism is then an integrated collection of physical processes that convert materials, energy and labour into finished products and wastes. This much of the industrial metabolism concept is straightforward, unproblematic and analytically helpful. What detracts from its utility, however, are:

- its conceptualisation in neo-classical economics terms of the mechanisms that regulate metabolic flows; and
- its preoccupation with productive systems divorced from the decision making context of the business enterprises that finance, operate and extract value and profits from those metabolic systems.

In the formulation of the metabolism concept by economists such as Robert Ayres, the regulation of flows through a system of production, transformation and consumption is achieved through a market derived price mechanism (Ayres et al., 1989). The price mechanism is postulated as balancing, on the one hand, the supply of products and, on the other hand, the demand for both products and labour. There are two problems with this set of propositions; first, do true market mechanisms actually exist that can effect this balance, and second, is it possible realistically to express all aspects of the industrial metabolic system in terms of prices, especially where environmental conditions are concerned?

To maintain that prices will balance the supply and demand of metabolic systems is to reassert the neo-classical stance that 'in the beginning there were markets'. Describing market mechanisms as 'Smithian virtues' Solow (1980) has graphically summarised the debate on this issue:

> Some of us see the Smithian virtues as needles in a haystack, as islands of measure zero in a sea of imperfections. Others see the imperfections as so many ticks on the hide of an ox, requiring only the occasional flick of its tail to be brushed away. (p.2)

Indeed, from the regulationist and power networks literatures (Peck and Tickell, 1991; Clegg, 1989), very different mechanisms can be envisaged as driving the dynamics of industrial metabolism that would deny the somewhat simplistic notions of balance and stability that are currently associated with the concept. The system could equally be interpreted as being driven by locally specific governance structure and modes of social regulation within which market mechanisms may play only a very minor part.

To express all aspects of the industrial metabolic system in terms of prices is equally problematic. Even if markets do exist, it is difficult to establish monetary prices for many environmental features and assets, such as wildlife, landscapes, wetlands, rivers and air quality. Jacobs (1994) has roundly criticised the contingent valuation approach that has been enthusiastically adopted in environmental economics which suggests that such prices can be and should be established for environmental features and qualities even when they are indisputably public goods. Harvey (1993) has pointed very clearly to the dilemma we face over money valuations of environmental assets:

> First, all the time we engage in commodity exchanges mediated by money ... it will be impossible in practice to avoid money valuations. Secondly, valuations of environmental assets in money terms, while highly problematic and seriously defective, are not an unmitigated evil. We cannot possibly know, however, how good the arbitrary valuations of 'nature' are (once we choose to go beyond the simple idea of an unpriced flow of goods and services) unless we have some alternative notion of value against which to judge the appropriateness or moral worth of money valuations. (p.9)

It might be concluded, therefore, that the incorporation of money valuations of environmental assets within the industrial metabolism framework is a 'least worst' solution. However, those money values are likely to inform regulatory mechanisms that are driven only partly, if at all, by market mechanisms.

The consequences of the neglect of the business enterprise within the industrial metabolism framework show very clearly in the context of the comprehensive studies that have been undertaken of the Rhine Basin (Ayres and Simonis, 1993; Stigliani and Anderberg, 1993; Stigliani et al., 1994). These studies have shown, for example, the extent and build up of cadmium pollution in different parts of the basin. However, by remaining 'disembodied' and divorced from the business enterprises involved in the zinc smelting from which most of the cadmium pollution derives, these studies (and the metabolism concept in general) have been unable to recognise the range of business strategies (some of them environmentally unfriendly) that can be adopted to accommodate the policy prescriptions derived from industrial metabolism analyses. Thus, reduced cadmium pollution levels in the Rhine Basin may not reflect greater environmental responsibility on the part of manufacturers but the shifting of polluting production to less regulated jurisdictions. Thus, environmental responsibility in one place may reflect no more than the export of polluting technologies to places that want industrialisation irrespective of the price (Taylor, 1995, forthcoming).

There is certainly evidence to support this point of view. It is only too clear in the export of toxic agricultural chemicals as aid from Germany to Albania (Edwards, 1995). It is evident in US chemical firms' search for locations free of environmental liabilities (including litigious communities), just as high environmental costs have been identified as a reason for the relocation of German chemicals firms to the US (Chowdhury, 1992; Johnson, 1988). However, it is not always easy to disentangle such an interpretation of industrial relocation and 'industry-flight' from business enterprises' search for locations offering comparative advantage on an international scale (Shin, 1993; Tattum, 1991). Indeed, Leonard (1988) has maintained that 'industry-flight' is a strategy applicable in very few industrial sectors and operating from pollution havens is a business strategy that offers only mixed success.

Industrial metabolism's balance sheet approach to the dynamic processes of chemicals transformation is appealing as a way of theorising and coming to grips with the processes promoting environmental degradation and change. Nevertheless, it is clear from the discussion that industrial metabolism needs to be grounded in the investment decision making context of the business enterprise. Its narrow dependence on market and price signals also needs to be broadened, not least because monetary values are difficult to attach to environmental assets (even through contingent valuation). However, to marry with the dynamic context of industrial metabolism and environmental change, the business enterprise also needs to be refined and situated in the dynamic context of network inequalities within which it must operate. Here the concepts of 'power networks' and 'circuits of power' are important analytical constructs, and these will be examined in the next two sections of the chapter.

Business enterprises and networks of power and inequality

In industrial and economic geography, the business enterprise is only now beginning to be conceptualised in a way that allows its relationship with the natural environment to be more fully appreciated. In the discipline's strong empiricist tradition business enterprises have tended to be classified into gross categories, while in the political economy approach they have often been treated in caricature, principally as the locus of the labour process (see Taylor, 1995). However, a fuller conceptualisation is emerging which places business enterprises into the much fuller networks of competing, controlling and complementary organisations and agents within which they must function (scc Taylor and Thrift, 1982 and 1983; Taylor, 1987 and 1995; Dicken and Thrift, 1992).

Within this power networks framework, the enterprise itself can be anything from a small family firm or partnership to a transnational corporation (TNC) or even a plant that is part of a large corporation or TNC. Each enterprise can be visualised as one point in a social economic constellation of points which must interact in order to extract value, make profits and survive. With some elements of the surrounding constellation the business enterprise will interact through buying and selling (a relationship of complementarity), while with others it will compete. With a third group it will be involved in relationships of control; with governments, unions, banks, professional organisations and corporate headquarter, for example. The realised relationships of a particular place and time will then constitute the business enterprise's 'task environment', and the many more potential relationships that are available to be realised at some other time have been labelled its 'domain'.

Central to the functioning of these actual or potential relationships is *inequality* involving dominance and subordination (McDermott and Taylor, 1982; Benson, 1975). This inequality in power has been ascribed to the control of resources such that:

> To survive in [a constellation of enterprises, organisations and agents, a business enterprise] ... must acquire and maintain resources (Pfeffer and Salancik, 1978). These resources ... include funds, personnel, information, products and services (Aldrich, 1972) which to Benson (1975) reduce to money [facilitating the execution of programmes of action] and authority [the right and responsibility to carry out those programmes] ... Control of resources ... endows related organisations and enterprises with different amounts of power and binds them into networks of unequal relationships. (Taylor, 1987, p. 213)

Control of resources makes some enterprises and parts of enterprises more powerful than others, focusing power networks on centres of strategic decision making (Cowling and Sugden, 1987; Dicken and Thrift, 1992).

What is defined in this power networks approach to the conceptualisation of business enterprise is, therefore, a 'topography' of asymmetric relationships between more powerful and less powerful agencies, in which key decision makers occupy the high ground. A static caricature of the forms that network inequality might take and the sorts of dominance that might be exercised in inter- and intra-organisational power networks was in fact developed a decade ago by Taylor and Thrift (1982, 1983) as an enterprise segmentation model. In that model, intra-organisational centrality and peripherality defined sub-units of large enterprises as 'leaders',

67

'intermediates', 'laggards' and 'supports', while on an inter-organisational scale increasing peripherality progressed from TNCs to multi-location enterprises and through a tail of legally autonomous smaller firms ranging from 'leader small firms' to the 'loyal opposition', 'satellites', 'satisfied small firms' and 'craftsmen'.

Associated with the functioning of these asymmetric power relationships are two competing (though arguably complementary) views of the forces that bind economic agents into networks. At one extreme is the 'undersocialised', economistic, transaction costs view based on efficiency principles derived from neoclassical economics (Williamson, 1975,1985; Zukin and DiMaggio, 1990). At the other extreme is the 'oversocialised', sociological view of enterprise 'embeddedness' which recognises explicitly the role of social forces in shaping economic agency (Granovetter, 1985; Powell, 1990; Zukin and DiMaggio, 1990; Grabher, 1993).

In the transaction costs model, relationships within and between enterprises are based almost exclusively on the costs of interaction. To quote Powell (1990):

> transactions that involve uncertainty about their outcomes, that recur frequently and require substantial "transaction-specific investments" - of money, time or energy that cannot be easily transferred - are more likely to take place within hierarchically organized firms. Exchanges that are straightforward, non-repetitive and require no transaction-specific investments will take place across a market interface. Hence transactions are moved out of markets into hierarchies as knowledge specific to transactions (asset specificity) builds up. When this occurs, the inefficiencies of bureaucratic organization are preferred to the relatively greater costs of market transactions. (p. 279)

The transaction cost model has been roundly criticised for, in effect, reducing all network relationships to issues of contracts and costs, and the identification of only two forms of governance - markets and hierarchies - has been labelled a 'disabling dichotomy' (Dicken and Thrift, 1992, p. 285). Nevertheless, the model does reinforce the importance of economic issues and processes in network relationships, even though it underplays the importance of inequality, dominance and subordination in those economic transactions. But, perhaps the most important limitation of the transaction cost model is that it strips the business enterprise from its social context and denies the development of trust and future expectations in the relationships between exchange partners (Grabher, 1993).

It is precisely the elements omitted from the transaction costs model that are central to the 'embeddedness' approach to enterprise network relationships. In this approach, economic exchange is seen as being embedded in a particular social structural context. This view is derived from the contention that ' ... the anonymous market of neoclassical models is virtually non-existent in economic life and transactions of all kinds are rife with [social connections].' (Granovetter, 1985, p. 495). Networks then are seen to ' ... serve as templates that channel market exchange; ... they facilitate collective action both within and outside market contexts.' (Zukin and DiMaggio, 1990, p. 20). Relational, reciprocal, open-ended and interdependent relationships are, in this interpretation of network relationships, seen as the antithesis of contracts, prices, routines, haggling and administrative fiat.

Thus, as specifications of the nature of business enterprise network relationships, the transaction costs and embeddedness interpretations stand in stark contrast. Against economism, the pursuit of efficiency and self interest is ranged interdependence, collaboration and reciprocity. But, are these positions so radically different? Are they instead differently focused views of the same broad sets of relationships that bind enterprises into functional networks - one economistic and the other sociological? It is after all well recognised that economic processes are socially and culturally constructed and that different societies and cultures operating within capitalism erect quite different and distinctive economic performance standards (Clegg, 1990; Christopherson, 1993).

There are clear geographical consequences attached to the functioning of the enterprise power networks discussed above. Indeed, it can be argued that while 'enterprise power' will affect 'place', 'place' will also affect 'enterprise power'. In turn, this reciprocal relationship will hold significant implications for interactions and interdependencies between 'economy' and the 'natural environment'.

There is substantial empirical evidence that network topographies, defined by unequal power relationships within and between business enterprises, have distinctive spatial implications (see the discussion in Taylor, 1995 and 1995 forthcoming). Peripheral members of power networks appear most concerned to exploit and mop up local market opportunities and much less concerned to act as export platforms to stimulate export-led growth. Their demand is also for mainly unskilled labour and they tend to stimulate the increased centralisation and agglomeration of productive activity at both the national and international scales.

Most importantly for the present discussion, peripherality in enterprise power networks appears to be associated with the slow or late acquisition of new technologies, further constraining the growth potential of those local enterprise ensembles in which peripheral enterprises predominate. New technologies tend to be developed at the core of enterprise networks (Caves, 1982; Dunning, 1986; Howells, 1990; Dicken, 1992), while those developed at network peripheries tend to be garnered by more central and powerful enterprises with obvious implications for the spatial relocation of growth potentials (Malecki, 1990, 1991). Over time, it would appear, new technologies are released from the central to the more peripheral network members, going first to subsidiaries in developed countries, then to subsidiaries in less developed countries, and much later and more slowly to joint ventures and arms-length licensees (Coughlin, 1983; Suzuki, 1993; Mansfield and Romeo, 1980). The implication of this evidence is that technology, and thus the relationship between an enterprise and the natural environment in terms of its use of materials and the manner in which it transforms and releases chemicals into the environment through production and consumption (i.e., its pollution signature), diffuses systematically across power networks from their cores to their peripheries. This process of diffusion is not intrinsically spatial but it has spatial implications which depend upon the ensembles of network members in places.

However, to counterbalance the potentially deterministic overtones of the impact of 'power' on 'place', it must also be remembered that 'place' will affect 'power' and enterprise centrality. Places and communities will certainly have ensembles of business enterprises that will endow them with distinctive growth potentials, but those particular capital:labour relationships will also create distinctive local commercial environments with different capacities and abilities to generate and attract business, investment and employment, and to cope with change. This is simply a reflection of the fact that business enterprise power networks are socially and culturally embedded (Granovetter, 1985), and the emerging regulationist perspective in economic geography affords a richer appreciation of the role of the state and local modes of social regulation as determinants of place-specific trajectories of economic change. From the perspective of impacts on the natural environment, communities can in effect accept or reject polluting activities, or at least create conditions that will attract or repel those activities.

To summarise, a business enterprise power networks perspective is emerging in economic geography, based on notions of power and inequality. Its chief characteristics have been summarised by Dicken and Thrift (1992):

> [P]roduction is organized primarily by business enterprises operating within extremely complex, dynamic networks of internalized and externalized transactional relationships of power and influence ... co-ordinated and effectively controlled by 'centres of strategic decision-making ... Business organizations, therefore, organize production systems ... but are themselves 'produced' through a complex historical process of embedding. (p. 287)

It has been contended here that this perspective offers a way of addressing the interaction between 'economy' and 'environment' in the realm of the concrete by focusing on technology, enterprise 'pollution signatures' and the mutual interrelationships between 'enterprise', 'power' and 'place'. Put simply, enterprise power networks define an organisational topography across which technology and pollution potentials diffuse, while local communities create conditions that can draw in or exclude those polluting activities. However, this approach has one major shortcoming - it is essentially *static*. It does not identify a dynamic of change: the ways in which network relationships alter and evolve; the dynamics of organisation and structure; shifts in technology and technical capabilities; changes in community attitudes and capacities; and of course shifting environmental potentials and vulnerabilities. It is argued here that the concept of 'circuits of power' developed by Stewart Clegg (1989) goes some way towards addressing these limitations of the static power networks framework.

Circuits of power and environmental change

The concept of circuits of power can be used to introduce mechanisms of change into the static topography of business enterprise power networks. The foundations of the approach are:

● the recognition of three concepts of power;
● the interpretation of these three concepts as interrelated circuits that will stimulate change;
● the twinning of power with resistance;
● recognition of the importance of rules and rule fixing procedures in the organisation of production; and
● the identification of disciplinary regimes, embracing empowerment and disempowerment, as sources of system instability.

Underpinning the concept is an extended interpretation of power, combining three quite separate conceptions of power in the context of the embedded firm (Clegg, 1989). First, there is the *agency view of power* (ascribed to Hobbes) in which power is commodified - something to be acquired. In this view, order is premised on sovereignty, which accords with the exercise of technical and positional power in resource dependence interpretation of organisational interrelationships (Pfeffer, 1981). Second, there is the Machiavellian view of *power as relationship*; concerned with what power does rather than what power is. Third, there is the Foucaudian view of *power as discipline* - the disciplinary practices of the state, society, culture and capital which generate and promote change and system instability. Through the processes involved in these circuits of power, the networks of relationships within which business enterprises are embedded are always in a state of dynamic tension in which short periods of change and

71

transformation punctuate what might be long periods of tolerated inequality.

It is important to recognise that the three circuits of power are not arranged hierarchically and that all impinge on agents and enterprises simultaneously. Therefore, care must be taken not to misinterpret the graphical representation of these circuits of power in Figure 4.1.

At a particular time and in a particular place, businesses enterprises (agencies) will interact one with another on a day-to-day basis within an established set of social relations. The control of 'money' and 'authority' (Benson, 1975) will be the basis of interaction within this *causal circuit of power* and the resulting inequalities and relationships of dominance and subordination will form the standing conditions of Figure 4.1. The negotiated or imposed inequalities involved in these standing conditions will generate time-specific and place-specific outcomes which will feed back through the circuit of power to affect the activities of agencies and to adjust social relations.

However, because the exercise of power provokes resistance, power will be exercised only episodically to create new standing conditions and to achieve new and modified outcomes. Both production and consumption require maximum certainty and minimised risk to create conditions of confidence. Under these circumstance, it is in the interest of all agencies to minimise the disruption to network relationships (no matter how unequal those relationships might be) which might be initiated by the exercise of power. The norm, therefore, will be long periods of network stability punctuated by short periods of upheaval. In terms of the relationship between economy and environment, patterns of material extraction and chemical release are likely, therefore, to remain stable for lengthy periods of time. It can be argued then that patterns of 'production pollution' and 'consumption pollution' across network topographies will have a tendency to persist irrespective of their environmental and ecological consequences.

However, the episodic agency of the *causal circuit of power* is also embedded within a 'field of forces' comprising a *dispositional circuit of power* relating to social integration and a *facilitative circuit of power* relating to system integration (Figure 4.1). To quote Clegg (1989):

> The circuit of social integration is concerned with fixing and refixing relations of meaning and of membership, while the circuit of system integration will be concerned with the empowerment and disempowerment of agencies' capacities, as these become more or less strategic as transformations occur which are incumbent upon changes in techniques of production and discipline. (p. 224)

The *dispositional circuit of power* is concerned with agent's attempts to stabilise outcomes. In the business enterprise context, they are looking for kindred spirits, with similar views or strategies, converts who can be persuaded to give their support, and others who can be intimidated into giving their support. Thus, social integration is achieved through the formulation and fixing of rules, the establishment of membership and by ascribing legitimacy and granting status to groups of agents. The process is entirely pragmatic and political - in other words, Machiavellian. It has been labelled the 'sociology of translation' and includes the process of 'enrolment' (Callon, 1986; Clegg, 1989). It creates what have been termed 'obligatory passage points' to ensure the continuation and stability of (unequal) outcomes in the causal or episodic circuit of power. In addition, it necessarily stimulates a tendency towards isomorphism and uniformity among agencies at one particular time and in one particular place as they all organise in the same way to achieve the same goal. These obligatory passage points can be seen in company law, labour laws and the full spectrum of 'system forming' and 'system guiding' government regulatory frameworks (Christopherson, 1993). They might also be identified as being affected by shifting social norms - modes of social regulation. In the context of environmental degradation, obligatory passage points can be seen not only in codified environmental regulation (where it is enforced) but in the persuasion and confrontation of environmental activists, and the pleas of environmental scientists for greater attention to be paid to their 'objective' wisdom (see Callon, 1986).

The *circuit of facilitative power* is concerned with system integration and the empowerment and disempowerment of agencies as techniques of production and discipline change through innovation managerial innovation and organisational innovation (Figure 4.1). Among business enterprises, different methods of production involve different forms of labour discipline and different work regimes. As those techniques of production and discipline change, the fixity and certainty sought through the creation of 'obligatory passage points' and the standing conditions of day-to-day operations is undermined. As it was put by Clegg (1989), the facilitative circuit is:

> ... a circuit of power which introduces a potent uncertainty and dynamism into power relations .. [It] is a source of new opportunities for undermining established configurations of episodic circuits of power, as it generates competitive pressure through new forms of technique, new forms of disciplinary power, new forms of empowerment and disempowerment. (p. 236)

This 'potent uncertainty' also has a spatial dimension as internationalising firms introduce new work regimes into the localities and communities they expand into.

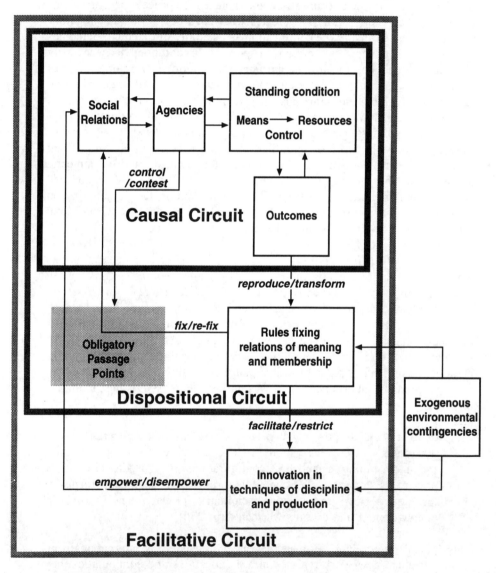

Figure 4.1 Circuits of Power (from Taylor, 1995)

The concept of 'circuits of power' outlined in this section adds detailed dynamic to the power networks framework outlined previously. It demonstrates an unequal day-to-day struggle between business enterprises based on their control of resources. It highlights attempts to achieve certainty and stabilised inequality through 'translation' and the erecting of 'obligatory passage points'. And it points to new technologies, new work regimes and new forms of discipline as forces of destabilisation. In short, it adds a dynamic tension to the relationships involved in enterprise power networks. Economy environment relationships seen from this power networks perspective are, therefore, in a constant state of flux as patterns and forms of production and consumption (and thus production and consumption pollution signatures) change.

Conclusions: networks, power and environmental change

The central tenet of the argument presented in this chapter is that the key to understanding the interconnectedness of economic and environmental change is the business enterprise which, when cast in the role of collective agency, embraces all economic actors from the self-employed to the transnational corporation. At a given point in time, production in its broadest sense is organised into networks of transactions and interactions involving competing, controlling and complementary organisations. The functioning of these networks of day-to-day interaction is dependent upon the control of resources and the achievement of socially, culturally and economically established performance criteria (of which profitability may be the most important but certainly not the only criterion). This is the *circuit of causal power* in which power is exercised only occasionally so that stability and certainty is maintained and production, consumption and investment is unhindered. These interactions are also embedded in locally specific frameworks of regulation, governance and modes of social regulation that modify and manipulate norms of production, consumption and performance and erect them as 'obligatory passage points'. In the *dispositional circuit of power*, obligatory passage points are established and maintained through the political processes of 'translation' and 'enrolment'; by co-opting, coercing or converting agencies to accept given norms of activity. Those obligatory passage points, specific to a certain time and a place, are also related to temporarily settled technologies of production, modes of organisation and disciplines of work, i.e., they are caught up in a *circuit of facilitative power*.

In such a temporarily stable system of production and consumption, with set technologies, enterprise forms, network configurations and systems of regulation, time-specific and place-specific systems of industrial metabolism will prevail. The systems of metabolism will have their own unique patterns of chemical release into the environment from both consumption and production - their own distinctive pollution signatures. These signatures will differ from place to place depending upon the nature of place-specific configurations of economic activities, frameworks of regulation and social constraints, coupled with the nature and extent of the diffusion of polluting technologies across business enterprise power networks (with the greatest pollution potential gravitating to network peripheries). The operation of standing conditions and obligatory passage points will tend to perpetuate these place-specific pollution signatures. However, technological change, changing work regimes and changing modes of discipline and regulation (*facilitative power*), either developed in situ or imported into a community through learning and inward investment, can radically alter these temporarily stable arrangements.

The inference is, therefore, that left to themselves, business enterprise power networks are incapable of acting to ameliorate mounting environmental problems locally and especially globally. All they can do it seems is seek to maintain the status quo, export polluting technologies to compliant jurisdictions or take flight. Only if a configuration of obligatory passage points can be created that forces them to adopt environmental sustainability as a goal and performance standard can environmental degradation be curbed. The question is whether technical knowledge (see Chapter 5 of this volume), environmental groups (see chapter 6 of this volume), policy interventions at all spatial scales (see Chapters 7, 8 and 9 of this volume), or simply market pressures (Clark, 1993) are capable of producing such a configuration. A cynic might argue that capitalism in its many varieties is incapable of developing a sustainable relationship with the physical environment.

Acknowledgements

This chapter has benefited greatly from discussions at the Moscow, Laxenburg and Fontainebleau meetings of the Human Dimensions of Global Change Working Group on Industrial Transformation and the Budapest meeting of the IGU Commission on the Organisation of Industrial Space. I am grateful to all the participants in those meetings, and hope that the process will continue. The arguments developed in this chapter draw significantly on Taylor (1995, forthcoming).

References

Aldrich, H.E. (1972), 'Technology and organizational structure: a re-examination of the findings of the Aston Group', *Administrative Science Quarterly*, vol. 17, pp. 26-43.

Ayres, R., Norberg-Bohm, V., Prince, J., Stigliani, W. and Yanowitz, J. (1989), *Industrial Metabolism, the Environment and Applications of Materials-Balance Principles for Selected Chemicals*, RR-89-11, IIASA, Laxenburg, Austria.

Ayres, R. and Simonis, U. (eds) (1993), *Industrial Metabolism: Restructuring and Sustainable Development*, The United Nations University Press, Tokyo.

Barbalet, J.M. (1985), 'Power and resistance', *British Journal of Sociology*, vol. 36, pp. 521-548.

Benson, J. K. (1975), 'The interorganisational network as a political economy', *Administrative Science Quarterly*, vol. 20, pp. 229-249.

Callon, M. (1986), ' Some elements of a sociology of translation: domestication of the scallops and the fishermen of St Brieuc Bay', in Law, J. (ed.) *Power, Action and Belief: A New Sociology of Knowledge?*, Sociological review Monograph 32, Routledge and Kegan Paul, London, pp. 196-233.

Caves, R. E. (1982), 'Multinational enterprise and technology transfer', in Rugman, E. (ed.), *New Theories of Multinational Enterprise*, Croom Helm, London, pp. 254-279.

Chowdhury, J. (1992), 'Plant siting (Part 1)', *Chemical Engineering*, vol. 99, pp. 28-31.

Christopherson, S. (1993), 'Market rules and territorial outcomes: the case of the United States', *International Journal of Urban and Regional Research*, vol. 17, pp. 274-289.

Clark, G.L. (1993), 'Global competition and the environmental performance of resource firms: is the "race to the bottom" inevitable?" paper presented to the OECD/NACEPT workshop on Environmental Policies and Industry Competitiveness, January, OECD, Paris.

Clark, W.C. (1988), 'The human dimension of global environmental change', in US Committee on Global Change, *Towards Understanding of Global Change*, National Academy Press, Washington DC, pp. 134-196.

Clegg, S. (1989), *Frameworks of Power*, Sage, London.

Clegg, S. (1990), *Modern Organizations: Organization Studies in the Postmodern World*, Sage, London.

Clegg, S. and Dunkerley, D. (1982), *Organization, Class and Control*, Routledge and Kegan Paul, London.

Cooke, P. (1989), 'The contested terrain of locality studies', *Tijdschrift voor Economische en Sociale Geographie*, vol. 80, pp. 14-29.

Coughlin, C.C. (1983), 'The relationship between foreign ownership and technology transfer', *Journal of Comparative Economics*, vol. 7, pp. 400-414.

Cowling, K. and Sugden, R. (1987), 'Market exchange and the concept of a transnational corporation', *British Review of Economic Issues*, vol. 9, pp. 57-68.

Cyert, R.M. and March J.G. (1963), *A Behavioral Theory of the Firm*, Prentice Hall, Englewood Cliffs, NJ.

Dicken, P. (1992), *Global Shift: The Internationalization of Economic Activity*, Second Edition, Paul Chapman Publishing, London.

Dicken, P. and Thrift, N. (1992), 'The organisation of production and the production of organisation: why business enterprises matter in the study if geographical industrialisation', *Transactions of the Institute of British Geographers, New Series*, vol. 17, pp. 279-281.

Dunford, M. (1995), 'Divergence, instability and exclusion: regional dynamics in Great Britain', paper presented to the Institute of British Geographers Conference, January, University of Northumbria.

Dunning, J.H. (1986), *Japanese Participation in British Industry*, Croom Helm, London.

Edwards, R. (1995), 'Dirty tricks in a dirty business', *New Scientist*, 18 February, pp. 12-13.

Grabher, G. (ed.) (1993), *The Embedded Firm: On the Socioeconomics of Industrial Networks*, Routledge, London.

Granovetter, M. (1985), 'Economic action and social structure: the problem of embeddedness', *American Journal of Sociology*, vol. 91(3), pp. 481-510.

Guelorget, Y., Jullien, V. and Weaver, P.M. (1993), 'A life cycle analysis of automobile tyres in France', Working Paper 93/67/EPS, Centre for the Management of Environmental Resources, INSEAD, Fontainebleu, France.

Handy, C. (1994), *The Empty Raincoat: Making Sense of the Future*. Hutchinson, London.

Harvey, D. (1993), 'The nature of the environment: the dialectics of social and environmental change', *Socialist Register, 1993, Real Problems False Situations*, Merlin Press, London, pp. 1-51.

Hesterberg, D., Stigliani, W.M. and Imeson, A.C. (1992), *Chemical Time Bombs: Linkages to Scenarios of Socioeconomic Development*, Executive Report 20, CTB Basic Document 2, IIASA, Laxenburg, Austria.

Howells, J. (1990), 'The internationalization of R&D and the development of global research networks', *Regional Studies*, vol. 24, pp. 495-512.

Jacobs, M. (1994), 'The limits to neoclassicism: towards an institutional environmental economics', in Redclift, M and Benton, T. (eds) *Social*

Theory and the Environment, Routledge, London, pp. 67-91.

Johnson, E. (1988), 'West Germany: the home market loses out to the US', *Chemical Week*, vol. 142, no. 24, pp. 22-25.

Johnston, R.J. (1989), *Environmental Problems: Nature, Economy and State*, Belhaven Press, London.

Leonard, H .J. (1988), *Pollution and the Struggle for World Product: Multinational Corporations, Environment and International Comparative Advantage*, Cambridge University Press, Cambridge.

Malecki, E. (1990), 'Technological innovation and paths to regional economic growth', in Schmandt, J. and Wilson, R. (eds) *Growth Policy in the Age of High Technology*, Unwin Hyman, Boston.

Malecki, E. (1991), *Technology and Economic Development: The Dynamics of Local Regional and National Change*, Longman, Harlow.

Mansfield, E. and Romeo, A. (1980), 'Technology transfer to overseas subsidiaries by US-based firms', *Quarterly Journal of Economics*, vol. 94, pp. 735-750.

Massey, D. (1984), *Spatial Divisions of Labour*, Macmillan, London.

McDermott, P. and Taylor, M. (1982), *Industrial Organisation and Location*, Cambridge University Press, Cambridge.

O'Riordan, T. (1981), *Environmentalism*, Pion, London.

O'Riordan, T. (1989), 'Contemporary environmentalism', in Gregory, D. and Walford, R. (eds) *Horizons in Human Geography*, Macmillan, Basingstoke, pp. 395-414.

Peck, J. and Tickell, A. (1991), *Regulation Theory and the Geographies of Spatial Accumulation; Transitions in Capitalism, Transitions in theory*, Spatial Policy Analysis Working Paper No. 12, School of Geography, University of Manchester.

Peet, R. and Thrift, N. (1989), 'Political economy and human geography', in Peet, R. and Thrift, N. (eds) *New Models in Geography, Volume I*, Unwin Hyman, London, pp. 3-29.

Perrow, C. (1990), 'Economic theories of organization' in Zukin, S. and DiMaggio, P. (eds) *Structures of Capital: The Organization of the Economy*, Cambridge University Press, Cambridge, pp. 121-152.

Pfeffer, J. (1981), *Power in Organisations*, Pitman, Marshfield MA.

Pfeffer, J. and Salancik, G. (1978), *The External Control of Organisations*, Harper and Row, New York.

Powell, W.W. (1990), 'Neither Markets nor hierarchies: network forms of organization', *Research in Organizational Behaviour*, vol. 12, pp. 295-336.

Redclift, M. and Benton, T. (1994), 'Introduction', in Redclift, M. and Benton, T. (eds) *Social Theory and the Global Environment*, Routledge, London, pp. 1-27.

Schoenberger, E. (1994), 'Corporate strategy and corporate strategists:

power, identity and knowledge within the firm', *Environment and Planning* A, vol. 26, pp. 435-451.

Scott, A. (1988a), *New Industrial Spaces*, Pion, London.

Scott, A. (1988b) *Metropolis: From the Division of Labour to Spatial Form*, University of California Press, Berkeley CA.

Shin, R. (1993), 'The dynamics of transboundary industrial location decisions: industrial flight or global strategy', *International Journal of Public Administration*, vol. 16, no. 4, pp. 443-465.

Socolow, R. (1994a), 'Preface', in Socolow, R., Andrews, C., Berkhout, F. and Thomas, V. (eds) *Industrial Ecology and Global change*, Cambridge University Press, Cambridge, pp. xv-xx.

Socolow, R. (1994b), 'Six perspectives from Industrial Ecology', in Socolow, R., Andrews, C., Berkhout, F. and Thomas, V. (eds) *Industrial Ecology and Global change*, Cambridge University Press, Cambridge, pp. 3-16.

Socolow, R., Andrews, C., Berkhout, F. and Thomas, V. (eds) (1994), *Industrial Ecology and Global change*, Cambridge University Press, Cambridge.

Solow, R. (1980), 'On theories of unemployment', *American Economic Review*, vol. 69, no. 4, pp. 1-16.

Storper, M. and Walker, R. (1983), 'The theory of labour and the theory of location', *International Journal of Urban and Regional Research*, vol. 7, pp. 1-43.

Storper, M. and Walker, R. (1984), 'The spatial division of labour: labour and the location of industries', in Sawyers, L. and Tabb, W. (eds) *Sunbelt/Snowbelt: Urban Development and Regional Restructuring*, Oxford University Press, New York, pp. 19-47.

Stigliani, W. (ed.) (1991), *Chemical Time Bombs: Definitions, Concepts and Examples*, Executive Report 16, CTB Basic Document 1, IIASA, Laxenburg, Austria.

Stigliani, W. and Anderberg, S. (1993), 'Industrial metabolism at the regional level: the Rhine basin', in Ayres, R. and Simonis, U. (eds) *Industrial Metabolism: Restructuring and Sustainable Development*, The United Nations University Press, Tokyo.

Stigliani, W. and Jaffe, P. (1993), *Industrial Metabolism and River Basin Studies: A New Approach for the Analysis of Chemical Pollution*, RR-93-6, IIASA, Laxenburg, Austria.

Stigliani, W., Jaffe, P. and Anderberg, S. (1994), 'Metals loading and the environment: cadmium in the Rhine basin', in Socolow, R., Andrews, C., Berkhout, F. and Thomas, V. (eds) *Industrial Ecology and Global change*, Cambridge University Press, Cambridge, pp. 287-296.

Suzuki, S. (1993), 'R and D spillover and technology transfer within vertical keiretsu groups: evidence from the Japanese electrical machinery industry, *International Journal of Industrial Organization*, vol. 11, pp. 573-591.

Tattum, L. (1991), 'Southern Europe: ready and waiting', *Chemical Week*, vol. 149, no. 9, pp. 20.

Taylor, M. (1987), 'Technological change and the business enterprise', in Brotchie, J., Hall, P. and Newton, P. (eds) *The Spatial Impact of Technological Change*, Croom Helm, London, pp. 208-228.

Taylor, M. (1995), 'The business enterprise, power and patterns of geographical industrialisation', in Conti, S., Malecki, E.J. and Oinas, P. (eds) *The Industrial Enterprise and Its Environment: Spatial Perspectives*, Avebury, Aldershot, pp. 99-122.

Taylor, M. (1995, forthcoming) 'Industrialisation, enterprise power and environmental change: an exploration of concepts', *Environment and Planning A*.

Taylor, M. and Thrift, N. (1982), 'Industrial linkage and the segmented economy, 1', *Environment and Planning A*, vol. 14, pp. 1601-1613.

Taylor, M. and Thrift, N. (1983), 'Business organisation, segmentation and location', *Regional Studies*, vol. 17, pp. 445-465.

The Economist Newspaper (1995), 'Reading the patterns', *The Economist*, vol. 335, No. 7908, pp. 109-111.

Tickell, A. and Peck, J. (1992), 'Accumulation, regulation and the geographies of post-Fordism: missing links in regulationist research', *Progress in Human Geography*, vol. 16, pp. 190-218.

Walker, R. (1989), 'A requiem for corporate geography: new directions in industrial organisation, the production of place and uneven development', *Geografiska Annaler*, vol. 71B, pp. 43-68.

Williamson, O.E. (1975), *Markets and Hierarchies: Analysis and Antitrust Implications*, Free Press, New York.

Williamson, O. E. (1985), *The Economic Institutions of Capitalism*, Free Press, New York.

Zukin, S. and DiMaggio, P. (1990), ' Introduction', in S. Zukin and P. DiMaggio (eds) *Structures of Capital: The Organization of the Economy*, Cambridge University Press, Cambridge, pp. 1-36.

5 Steering the eco-transition: A material accounts approach

Paul M. Weaver

Introduction

The environment has become a major public concern and much attention is now devoted to mitigating anthropogenic environmental impacts. Industrial economic activities are under special scrutiny since these are the principal generators of environmental damage. This damage is largely (though not exclusively) a function of the materials throughput of the industrial economy. A commitment to undertake a fundamental revision of the industrial economic system is establishing, and the industrialised world stands poised to undergo an environmentally motivated 'eco' transition. This will be both policy and market driven.

The issues to which eco-transition gives rise are much more than environmental. Eco-transition represents a potentially major economic upheaval involving fundamental systemic changes in response to changing societal values and concerns. It presents both threats and opportunities for business, policy makers and society. It raises concerns about employment impacts, profitability, competitiveness, and trade; about financing development and risk taking; about the direction of technological progress; and about environmental policy impacts on all of these as well as on the environment. Ideally, eco-transition processes should be consensual. This requires that outcomes, including distributional effects, are clear and transparent. Eco-transition pathways should be as effective and efficient as possible.

Such concerns raise several questions. Which private and public sector actions are likely to be most effective in limiting environmental damage? How might synergies be developed and captured so that actions to protect the environment might help achieve other societal objectives? How can we protect against environmental policies being used or manipulated to secure unfair industrial or trading advantage or to shift environmental damage from one type, medium or place to another? How can we best clarify and reconcile inevitable trade-offs such as between short term and long term approaches to environmental protection?

In this chapter, it is argued that a necessary starting point for relevant analysis is to account for industrial economic activities in materials terms. Against this criterion, most conventional frameworks for analysing industrial economic activities, including those used by geographers, are inadequate. Almost exclusively, conventional frameworks for analysis are based upon economic theory, models and methods. These lack any explicit treatment of the environment. However, relevant approaches to materials accounting are being developed and applied in emerging, interdisciplinary fields such as industrial ecology. These include input-output methods, eco-balances, eco-profile analyses and product life cycle assessments. The aim of this chapter is briefly to describe these methods and their philosophical underpinnings. It is also argued that much could be gained if geographers were to adopt, further develop and combine these methods with more familiar analytical approaches of economic geography. To illustrate the ideas explored in this chapter, results from an ongoing study of eco-transition in the European pulpwood, pulp and paper sector are summarised.

Why materials matter

A basic proposition of environmental concern is that long term human welfare depends upon human activity achieving a sustainable balance with the physical and biological subsystems: the atmosphere, hydrosphere, lithosphere, and biosphere. These subsystems (each a natural reservoir for materials) have evolved over eons into a complex and stable interrelationship. Human activities, and especially industrial activities, are now perturbing that relationship in significant ways, especially by increasing the flux of materials between subsystems and the holdings of materials within individual reservoirs. The mining of substances for industrial use, for example, means that material formerly held underground in long-lived structures (rock), is freed. Whether the material (e.g. sulphur) is embodied temporarily in an economically useful product (e.g. vulcanized rubber), an interim product (e.g. sulphuric acid), or lost almost immediately as a pollutant (e.g. sulphur dioxide), it will eventually enter and accumulate in natural reservoirs (the atmosphere, lakes, soils etc.) other than those from which it was obtained.[1]

Several categories of effect are possible. Some materials have particular chemical, physical, or biological properties. Sulphur is acidifying. Carbon dioxide released to the atmosphere from the mining and burning of fossil fuels has radiative (physical) properties that differ from those of other atmospheric gases. Heavy metals such as lead and cadmium are intrinsically toxic to many biological organisms. Their presence in biologically available form threatens a potential interference in biological processes. Since biological processes mediate the natural fluxes of matter between reservoirs (through the grand nutrient cycles) and ensure a quasi steady state environment, such interference is potentially destabilising.

By design or by default, raw materials may be transformed into entirely new states by industrial economic processes; i.e., states that do not occur in nature. The ozone destroying refrigerants and propellants known as chloro-fluoro-carbons (CFCs) constitute such a category. They were produced by design. Many highly toxic, halogenated, organic compounds (e.g. dioxins), which also would not naturally occur, are produced and released incidentally. Even materials that represent no obvious problem on release may have potential for further transformation and for future environmental disturbance. Still others may catalyse reactions or processes. Acids, for example, can mobilise heavy metals, increasing their bio-availability (Stigliani et al., 1991).

The natural balance between physical and biological subsystems and reservoirs is now significantly perturbed by human activities. Several studies have compared reservoir holdings and fluxes of particular materials for the pre- and post industrialisation periods and have shown major differences (e.g. for heavy metals see Galloway et al., 1982; for nitrogen see Ayres et al., 1994). Greenhouse gases are accumulating in the atmosphere. Toxic heavy metals are accumulating in soils and sediments. Soils and fresh-water stocks are being acidified. Some of these problems are of local, some of regional and a few of global scale and significance. Global scale environmental impacts are most evident when human activities affect the flux of materials between the solid (lithospheric) and liquid (oceanic and atmospheric) reservoirs. The atmosphere is especially prone. It comprises relatively little material so its composition is soon affected by pollutants. It is also the most fluid reservoir, which gives potential for very rapid mixing and long distance transport of materials both horizontally and vertically. This gives the capacity to induce global scale problems such as a breakdown of the protective stratospheric ozone layer and potential climatic change. Other potential global scale problems may be slower to develop and less immediately obvious. The grand nutrient cycles, for example, are far out of balance, although the full significance of this is not yet known.

The character of industry

In terms of materials throughput[2], patterns of industrial activity across the globe are characterised by overriding uniformity. They are materials intensive and 'leaky'. As to the first, steady materials efficiency

85

improvements per unit of economic value added have been recorded (e.g. Jänicke et al., 1988). Nonetheless, materials efficiency gains are seldom translated into overall reductions in materials use and are usually more than offset by increases in the volume of goods and services produced and consumed.[3] Total materials mobilisation by the global industrial economy continues to increase and it is this, together with projected further increases if expected global development continues along a 'business-as-usual' pathway, that gives rise to much of the current environmental concern.[4] The 'leaky' aspect is not just because of pollutants released at industrial sites, as is sometimes supposed. In fact, such releases have been significantly reduced. Rather, it is because materials that leave industrial sites as products are virtually all ultimately released, one way or another, into the environment. Many products are designed to be used dissipatively (for example, fuels, pesticides, fertilizers, aerosols, paints and most other 'consumables'). Their loss to the environment is thus assured.[5] Other products, durable goods such as cars and refrigerators, have longer economically useful lives. Nonetheless, when such products are worn out they are discarded. Unless specifically recovered, which is seldom the case, the materials that they embody become 'wastes'. These are mostly buried at land-fills or incinerated. Overall, we can be sure that, in amount and elemental composition, the annual total release of materials to the environment must broadly equal the annual total draw on virgin materials; i.e., the product of all extractive industry (mining, quarrying, drilling, pumping, etc.) is ultimately released back into the environment.

Key eco-transition issues

The materials throughput of our industrial economies is a result of our technological choices and the structure of industry in terms of the mix of the technologies used. In turn, these are the result of a complex interplay between competitive market forces, power relationships among economic and political actors and the regulatory/policy framework. This interplay has long been of interest to industrial geographers for reasons other than understanding its environmental consequences. Now, however, concern is focusing ever more strongly upon the environmental impacts of economic activities and how these might be moderated. The basic directions for change will be towards de-materialisation and detoxification of the economy; i.e., toward a decoupling of economic value added from materials loss (especially, loss of toxic materials). However, the mechanisms for inducing this change have still to be clarified. Moreover, change could follow any of several courses.

At one extreme, the transition pathways (whether for particular industries, for whole economies or in respect to the delivery of a particular end use product or service) could be rapid, efficient and effective. They could yield improved environmental performance while protecting or increasing employment opportunities, profitability, competitiveness, living conditions, local and regional equity and local self-determination and self-sufficiency. At the other extreme, they could be slow, inefficient and ineffective. There are real grounds for concern since perverse environmental outcomes from the transition are possible. The transition process, especially to the extent that this is policy led, is particularly open and vulnerable to manipulation by interest groups. There is also a danger that the necessary transition might be frustrated or jeopardised by indecision over what constitutes an appropriate strategic direction.

Problems have already arisen. In some instances, measures taken ostensibly to provide protection for the environment (even measures advocated by green groups) may have had perverse environmental outcomes. Greenpeace's campaign to require that cars sold in European markets be equipped with catalytic converters to reduce noxious emissions is a case in point. Greenpeace ran a successful campaign that led to the European Union (EU) legislating the use of catalytic converter technology. Subsequent work has demonstrated that the environmental stress caused by obtaining the materials used to make the converters, together with that caused during converter manufacture and use, may be greater than the environmental benefits obtained by their use.[6] The sting in the tail is that the principal target for the Greenpeace campaign was the Ford Motor Company. Ford resisted pressure to introduce catalytic converters, favouring instead the development of its alternative, lean burn engine technology. This, Ford claimed, would have reduced emissions at source. Greenpeace's successful campaign led to Ford abandoning its alternative technological direction, albeit that this would now seem to have been the more promising from an environmental standpoint (Gabel, 1990 and 1991).

An example of possible manipulation of environmental policy by vested interests is provided by US experience in respect to CFCs. There is a suggestion, for example, that concern over the effect of CFC releases on the stratospheric ozone layer was, at one stage, turned to the positive commercial advantage of the established CFC manufacturers. The manufacturers (Dupont and ICI) agreed voluntary production ceilings among themselves and the responsible US governmental agencies in respect to the US market. These ceilings, while restricting annual sales of CFCs in the US, made no provision in the beginning for the withdrawal of CFC technology. Rather, they secured a US market for the substances, provided protection for established producers against new market entrants and allowed prices to rise. The established CFC industry was thus able to exploit environmental concern to increase profitability from one of its more environmentally damaging operations (Gabel, 1992).

87

A new situation is now emerging in respect to policy making within the European pulp and paper industry which threatens to embrace the worst aspects of both of the previously discussed cases. The concern arises from a set of measures aimed at mandating or otherwise influencing the level of secondary fibre use in specific paper grades. The measures include set minimum requirements on fibre recovery and reuse, eco-taxes on virgin pulp and eco-labelling schemes that favour the use of secondary over primary fibre. Fibre recycling is being promoted even though it is not yet clearly established whether or under what circumstances the use of recycled fibre in preference to virgin pulp is most environmentally benign. Concerns have been raised that recycling might increase the rate of build up of greenhouse gases in the atmosphere and have damaging effects on European forests (Virtanen and Nilsson, 1992). Just as lean burn engine technology was effectively locked-out by catalytic converter legislation, reservations have been expressed over the effects of fibre recycling policy on the long term development of environmentally improved primary pulping and energy recovery technologies (Weaver, 1994a). Whatever the environmental implications of fibre recovery and re-use, greater fibre recycling would favour some industrial and trading interests over others (Weaver, 1994b). There is circumstantial evidence to suggest that it is being actively promoted by the potential beneficiaries. This case will be returned to later.

These examples serve to illustrate that there is need to establish the basis of an eco-transition strategy on scientific grounds. Key issues are concerned with:

- widening the technological choice set;
- modifying and influencing the processes by which technology choices are made;
- attaining synergies between a reduction in environmental impact and the achievement of other societal objectives;
- maintaining a level playing field for competition;
- avoiding adverse distributional consequences; and,
- avoiding perverse environmental outcomes.

Achieving a 'successful' eco-transition will depend heavily upon our capacity: to establish which sectors and what kinds of industrial activities ought to be promoted, and which would need to be phased out on grounds of fundamental environmental incompatibility; to capitalise on the positive thrust of technological development within those sectors that will play an increasing role in the future economy; and to evaluate environmental impacts caused directly (for example, by technologies) and indirectly (for example, by policies that influence technology choices).

Limitations of approaches derived from economics

If these are some of the issues and concerns, how well placed is the research community to provide guidance on eco-transition processes? This depends upon how relevant to an environmental assessment of eco-transition processes and pathways we consider our existing bodies of knowledge, theory and analytical methods to be. Much of our expertise in this area (even as industrial geographers) derives from conventional economics, which characterises the industrial economic system in money terms. The industrial economic system is visualised in terms of stocks, flows and processes. The processes - production, consumption and exchange - are interconnected by flows of inputs and outputs. Inputs and outputs have values represented by prices. The motivation for production, consumption and exchange is to add value.

A basic limitation with this characterisation of an economy is that prices generally fail to distinguish adequately between two fundamentally different sets of economic inputs and outputs; those that embody physical materials and those that do not. If industrial activity is characterised as an economic process by which value is added as resources are transformed into goods, it is also a physico-chemical process that uses energy to transform material inputs into useful products and releases waste materials back into the environment. As we have argued, this is the basic link between industrial economic activity and the environment. Since much of industrial and economic geography follows directly from conventional economics, it shares the limitations that derive from reducing economic activities to money terms. When the material and non-material are treated as equivalent, the environmental disturbance implications of different system configurations (different geographies and technologies of production, consumption, waste management and exchange) are not captured.

To capture what is environmentally relevant, we need a materials mobilisation and transformation characterisation of industrial economic systems to parallel the economic characterisation. We also need an understanding of the capacity of ecosystems as sources and sinks for materials.

Industrial ecology

Industrial ecology has grown up as a field of science to study the relationships between our current materials intensive and leaky industrial economic systems and those ecosystems and organisms affected by the extraction of materials and the receipt of wastes. Industrial ecology is 'the study of man-made industrial systems in which the ecological patterns and functions of natural systems are used as a framework for managing the use and flows of materials and energy with the goal of creating interlocking and sustainable industrial systems' (Frosch and Galloopulus, 1989). The analytical frameworks of industrial ecology include a range of concepts and tools. Two such concepts are the notion of an industrial 'metabolism' and the potential existence of future 'industrial ecosystems'.

Several analysts have drawn analogies between the internal processes of firms and those of organisms (Ayres and Simonis, 1994). Both firms and organisms process materials into useful forms using an external source of available energy. Both are examples of 'self-organising dissipative systems' (Ayres, 1988) that maintain a stable state condition far from thermodynamic equilibrium. Manufacturing firms use energy to convert material inputs into useful products. In the process, they additionally generate wastes. Organisms ingest food, which provides both energy and materials for maintenance, growth and reproduction. They, too, generate wastes. The 'metabolism' metaphor can be identified at several other levels; for example, at industry level and at the level of economic regions. At the highest level it is applicable to the whole industrial economic system. The counterpart, at this level, is the global ecosystem.

It is at this highest level that a critical and revealing difference in the fundamental operational character of the relevant internal systems is most apparent. An ecosystem recycles materials internally. Energy derived from the sun and captured by primary producers (plants) through photosynthesis is passed on through the food chain. Nutrients taken up by primary producers are similarly passed on. Biological organisms are involved in complex interaction with the abiotic elements of ecosystems, in particular with the grand nutrient cycles. In time frames of concern to humans, materials mobilised and transformed by the global ecosystem are continuously recycled. The waste output from one process becomes the material input to another. In contrast, our current industrial economic systems continuously draw on new materials. Only a small fraction of the material mobilised is recovered and re-used.

This fundamental difference provides important operational principles and goals to guide an eco-transition. A goal might be for our industrial-economic systems to try to replicate the organisational structures of ecosystems or to become embedded within them in ways that achieve an essentially closed materials cycle. The idea would be to create 'industrial ecosystems' (NAS, 1994) in which reliance on extractive resources and emission of wastes would be reduced to levels consistent with the capacity of the environment to supply those materials and to process those wastes on a renewable basis. The draw on extractive resources would be reduced to the level needed to replace inevitable dissipative losses. Companies would 'eat' each other's and societies' wastes (Frosch and Galloopulus, 1989). The scope for pollution prevention, waste reduction and recycling clearly increases as the search extends beyond the immediate product or process. Opportunities for waste reduction and recycling may be found within companies, between companies, within industrial parks and within the national, regional and global economy.[7]

The process of achieving an ecotransition involves structural economic change. Simonis sets out some of the relevant structural elements that we might want to consider:

> The expression 'structural change' or 'restructuring' is generally used to characterise the decline or increase over time in certain sectors, groups of industries, or regions (and sometimes technologies) as regards gross national/domestic product. One may also think of structural change in terms of a transition in the mix of goods and services produced; or one may refer to a broader set of changes in the economy, not only in its products and employment, but also in the social relations of production (e.g., unionisation, part-time versus full-time jobs), the means of production (handicrafts, robotics), and the forces of production (market demand, profits)... Economic restructuring thus subsumes industrial restructuring... Any restructuring of the sectors (or industries) in an economy is, of course, linked to more profound changes in other realms... the regional structure, the employment structure and the investment structure. All of these might be quite relevant in explaining the given environmental situation of a country, or its change over time' (Simonis, 1994, p. 32)

In explaining the environmental situation, Simonis therefore distinguishes between direct and indirect influences. In determining materials use by our industrial economic systems, the direct influence is through technology. If we characterise the industrial economic system as one producing a wide range of valued goods and services, many of which can be delivered using alternative technologies, environmental disturbance per unit of production or consumption is directly a function of the 'technology structure' defined by:

- the mix of goods and services demanded within an economy;
- the mix of technologies used within an economy throughout all the different stages in the materials 'life cycle' (including materials sourcing, processing, manufacturing, transport, recycling and disposal);
- the environmental disturbance potential associated with each technology; and
- the geography of production, consumption and waste management.

Indirectly, environmental disturbance is a function of whatever forces are relevant to explaining or changing this technology structure.

Tools for analysis

As well as providing useful concepts, industrial ecology also provides a range of tools for analysis of the industrial economic system based upon materials accounting. The basis for this is inventory analysis; the preparation of balanced inventories of material inputs and outputs. Inventories (sometimes called materials or eco-balances) can be developed for factories, firms, industries or regions. More typically, however, they are developed for specific unit processes. The notion of the division of economic activities (especially production) into 'unit' processes is well established and derives from chemical engineering practice. A unit process involves a materials transformation. It is characterised by a set of inputs and outputs, including one unit mass of a main product (or several co-products). The inputs include feedstocks and energy. The outputs include products and wastes. The term 'balance' is used since inputs and outputs should be equal in mass terms both at the aggregate and elemental levels.

Unit processes can be combined in many ways to reflect how materials flow through our industrial economic systems. A composite process chain or set of chains describes the conversion of a set of primary materials into a single finished material. When different processes are available to perform any specific materials transformation, a composite process chain can be constructed to reflect the mix of processes that best characterises the industry. Figure 5.1 provides an example of a composite process chain, in this case for the production of bleached kraft pulp. Composite process chains combine all inputs and outputs associated with the derivation of raw materials, pre-production, production and transportation in respect to the finished material considered; i.e., production plus all relevant upstream processes. Inputs and outputs associated with upstream processes involved in the chain are accounted for on a pro-rated basis to derive an eco-balance for the finished material (Table 5.1).

A life cycle is a 'cradle-to-grave' analysis of material inputs and outputs associated with the delivery of economic value. This could be in the form of either goods or services. As well as the production (supply) side of industrial-economic activities, life cycle assessment includes the consumption (demand) and disposal (return to nature) side. Materials are tracked from their origins in the environment, through to their return there as wastes. All inputs and outputs incurred are inventoried and an eco-balance prepared on a unit product/service basis. Life cycle assessment also makes provision to account for feed-back loops, such as those implied by materials recovery and reuse. Figure 5.2 provides a simplified example of the paper life cycle. Table 5.2 gives an eco-balance for the life-cycle associated with a product - paper.

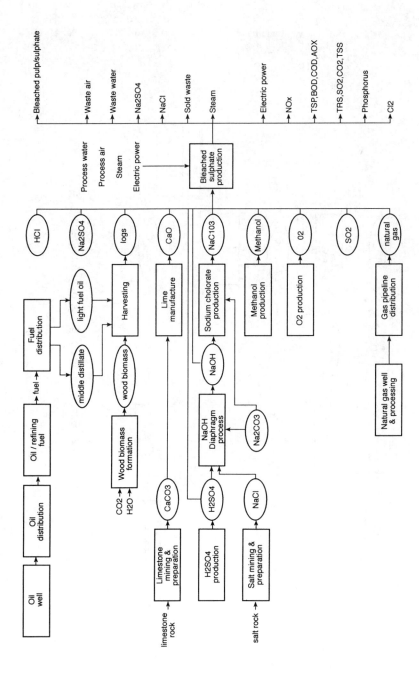

Figure 5.1   Example of a composite process chain for bleached sulphate (kraft) pulp

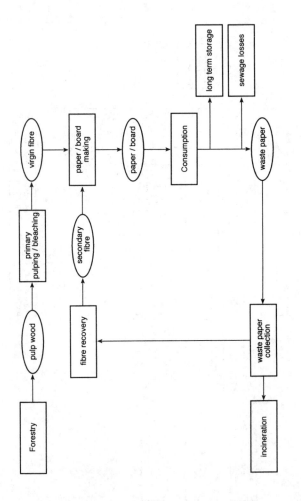

Figure 5.2 Simplified life cycle of pulp and paper

Table 5.1
Ecobalance for bleached kraft (sulphate) pulp (per kg pulp)

INPUTS			OUTPUTS		
Used Materials			**Emissions to Air**		
Wood	Kg	2.2			
Water	l	54.0	Dust	g	1.60
CaO	g	7.0	CO	g	2.30
Cl_2	g	15.0	NO_x	g	1.30
$H_2 SO_4$	g	18.0	SO_2	g	2.40
Na ClO_3	g	18.0	Mercaptans	g	0.27
Na OH	g	24.0	H_2S	g	0.02
O_2	g	16.0			
Peroxides	g	2.2	**Emissions to Water**		
SO_2	g	11.0			
Energy			Water	l	54.00
			Solids	g	0.300
Input Material	MJ	33.0	Salts	g	48.00
Lumbering	MJ	0.40	Chlorides	g	20.00
[Net] Process	MJ	0.00	COD	g	22.00
	kWh	-0.05	BOD	g	1.00
			AOX	g	0.90
Transport			Sulphides	g	No data
Rail	km	100	**Solid Wastes**		
Truck	km	100			
			Sludge	g	48.0

Source: Adapted from BUWAL (1991).

Table 5.2

Ecobalance of kraft standard bleached/coated paper (per kg paper)

INPUTS

Sulphate bleached pulp	g	770.0
Kaolin	g	265.0
adjuvants	g	0.4
Energy	MJ	35.9
	kWh	1.4
Water	l	63.1

OUTPUTS

TO AIR			TO WATER			TO LAND		
Particles	g	2.7	Water	l	63.1	Solid waste	g	160
CO	g	2.9	Fibres	g	1.43			
HC	g	6.5	Dissolved Solids	g	2.20			
NO_x	g	5.6	Suspended Solids	g	0.001			
N_2O	g	0.4	BOD	g	2.47			
SO_2	g	10.9	COD	g	20.84			
Aldehydes	mg	9.5	AOX	g	0.69			
Other organic			Ammonia	mg	0.89			
compounds	mg	15.6	Chlorides	g	15.42			
NH_3	mg	3.4	Fluorides	mg	1.923			
Fluorides	mg	0.01	Hg	mg	0.001			
Cl_2	mg	0.01	Oils	g	0.031			
Hg	mg	0.02	Phenols	mg	0.00			
H_2SO_4	g	0.07	Salts	g	36.96			
Mercaptons	g	0.21	Sulphide	g	0.00			
H_2S	g	0.02						

Source: Adapted from BUWAL (1991)

Once derived, eco-balances can be classified. Different inputs and outputs can be reviewed against a profile of environmental and human health problems to which they might contribute: the build-up of atmospheric greenhouse gases, environmental acidification, environmental nutrification, eco- and human toxicity and so on. Several systems for comparing the relative contributions of different emissions to particular forms of damage - effect scores - have been developed (e.g., BUWAL, 1991; CSG/Tellus, 1992; Heijungs, 1992). Different systems exist because, by implication, these cannot be definitive. Any system of fixed weights cannot capture the non-linearities that characterise the relation between emissions and environmental damage. This is an active area of continuing research, with much effort being expended to define improved systems for calculating environmental disturbance potential. In the meantime, surrogates like the CML system are widely used. Classification of the eco-balance and its evaluation using such a system gives the eco-profile of environmental effect scores across the set of problems considered.

A final stage can be to evaluate an overall environmental effect by normalising the effect scores, defining weights that reflect the relative importance of the different problems considered, and determining a weighted average effect score. Clearly, this is also a subjective process in that it depends upon value judgements about the relative importance of different kinds of problem.[8] Nonetheless, it is useful since it enables comparison to be made between, for example, the life cycle environmental impacts of different products that deliver equivalent end user services (e.g. of metal, plastic, glass and paper packaging materials) and of alternative product life cycles (e.g. based upon using different production processes, feedstocks or levels of materials recycling). It can also be used as the basis for life cycle optimisation. Since we are concerned to reduce environmental disturbance relative to each unit of economic value added, we can also use overall environmental impact scores as a basis for comparing environmental disturbance productivities and for charting progress in reducing materials and waste intensities. Figure 5.3 illustrates the different stages of life cycle assessment.[9]

An illustration: the pulp and paper sector

We can illustrate the application of materials accounting methods to issues of eco-transition by referring to an ongoing study of the pulp and paper sector. Here, we briefly describe the issues, methods employed, preliminary results and their implications (see Weaver et al., 1995, for a fuller report).

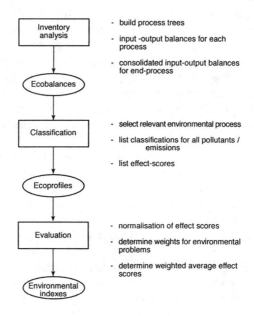

Figure 5.3 Possible components of a life cycle assessment

Issues

Pulpwood, pulp and paper has traditionally been vilified as one of our most environmentally damaging industries. Yet the industry has made great strides in reducing its environmental impact. Also, it is potentially one of the most environmentally benign industries since its principal material input, pulpwood, is a renewable resource.

This potential for improvement raises several questions. What are the short and long term limits to the industry's environmental impact and what steps from both public policy bodies and the private sector are necessary to achieve them? What are the most significant industrial and international trade implications of a more sustainable product life cycle configuration? And, how might these help or hinder progress toward the achievement of that configuration?

Approach

To explore these questions for the European pulpwood, pulp and paper industry materials accounting methods (used to analyse environmental impacts associated with different technologies and commodities) were combined with a flow model of the European industry (used to recognise flows of primary materials and mass commodities between major European countries and blocs). Optimisation methods were applied to solve the model. The goal was to search all feasible configurations of the industry for ones that are the least environmentally damaging yet which satisfy a set of constraints including meeting the demand for paper and board products, industrial capacity constraints and maximum secondary fibre recovery rates. The model allowed examination of the environmental consequences and impact on the optimal industry configuration under different assumptions about technologies, weightings of different environmental problems, regulatory policies, and so on.

Results

Optimality is a function of technological performance, the geography of the sector and the scheme used to evaluate environmental impacts of different type. We assumed one evaluation scheme for base runs of the model. Given the current environmental performance of different technologies (for primary and secondary pulp production, incineration, transportation, etc.), the optimal configuration for the European industry based upon our evaluation scheme is consistent with maximum feasible recycling, although the environmental gain is a decreasing function of the recycling rate. Shifting to this configuration would diminish by about one third the industry's environmental impact in respect to the processes considered by the model.

This is not a surprising result, and it apparently vindicates current public policy emphasis on recycling. However, the result is very sensitive to the environmental performance of the various production processes and incineration technologies. The industry is characterised by sharp technological improvement thresholds which can render maximum recycling no longer the optimal policy. If these technology thresholds can be achieved (which may be possible through innovation), higher levels of primary pulping, less recycling and more incineration of waste paper for energy recovery would be the better strategy.

If a maximum recycling approach is adopted, the optimum configuration for the industry would involve geographical specialisation in production. The residual demand for virgin fibre (which will always exist) should be met by those countries with the most environmentally benign primary pulping technologies and in integrated pulp and paper mills. To reduce unnecessary transport, virgin pulp would not be traded. Only paper products would enter trade, and trade would be dominated by high quality grades containing mostly (if not entirely) virgin fibre. Post-consumption waste from these papers

99

would ultimately become source material for fibre recovery in the consumer countries. Waste paper would never be traded.

Interestingly, while the optimal outcome is sensitive to the environmental performance of particular technologies we found it to be rather insensitive to different schemes used for evaluating environmental damages. This is important because of the controversy surrounding any such evaluation scheme. It implies that the substantive findings of the research are likely to be correct in general if not in detail. For example, the optimal configuration is robust to different weights applied when aggregating different kinds of environmental harm.

Implications

There are several important implications of these results which can briefly be commented upon. One derives from evidence that current public policy, with its emphasis on maximising recycling, may be reducing the investment funds needed for maintaining forests and for introducing improved environmental technologies for virgin pulp production. Maximum recycling takes market share away from primary pulp producers. There is also evidence that uncertainty about future policy direction is creating a generally unfavourable investment climate around the industry. Our findings indicate that this policy direction might be shortsighted in that it risks locking in today's best available technology while locking out new technologies which, in the long run, might be environmentally preferred.

A second important implication is that the choice between maximum feasible recycling (today's best approach), and improved production of virgin pulp with energy recovery (perhaps tomorrow's best approach), has major international trade repercussions. For example, maximum recycling is an equilibrium in which Scandinavian countries supply all of Europe's residual need for virgin fibre, not by exporting it but by exporting paper grades based on virgin pulp. Consuming countries, such as Germany, would produce no virgin fibre but would focus on fibre recovery and the production of lower paper and board grades. By contrast, with improved pulping process technologies, the optimal configuration entails the greater self-sufficiency of individual European countries with widespread production and use of pulpwood, virgin pulp and paper, less recycling and greater incineration of waste paper with energy recovery.

These two implications suggest a third. Although the trade consequences of alternative environmental policy trajectories have never previously been quantified, public policy makers at the national level and industrialists are undoubtedly generally aware of them. This provides a motive for them to manipulate the public policy process. While we cannot confirm that environmental policy is heavily influenced by trade and industry concerns (although this is frequently alleged), we are able to demonstrate that the environmental policy positions taken by particular states are consistent with their trade and industry interests. By providing a formal quantitative model to analyse both environment and trade issues, we are able to look explicitly at this potential environment-trade policy conflict. We are also able to look at issues surrounding the policy making process itself; for example, about how best to operationalise the subsidiarity principle in the context of environmental policy making (Weaver, 1994b).

Finally, the study has implications for policy. Specifically, it implies that policies to promote recycling should not mandate secondary fibre components uniformly across all paper grades. Rather, the paper market should be differentiated, with some of high quality printing grades always being made exclusively (or almost exclusively) from virgin fibre. Current suggestions to extend legislation on secondary fibre components to printing grades should be resisted on this basis. More generally, the study demonstrates a well known point, but one that needs quantification and repeated emphasis, that command and control policies that specify particular technologies are likely to be less efficient in comparison with flexible policies that set up incentives to invest in improved technologies.

Conclusions

Finding ways of bringing about an effective, efficient and fair eco-transition implies a major interdisciplinary research agenda in which geographers have a clear stake. Eco-transition will alter the geography of production and consumption, the geography of technology, patterns of trade and international competitiveness. As the pulp and paper case study demonstrates, environmental policy choices will directly affect markets, R&D, innovation, investment, employment and trade, as well as the environment. These aspects will become increasingly topical as policy making shifts further toward an approach based upon manipulating product life cycles. The issues implied offer a wholly new and important industrial-geographic research agenda. A materials based characterisation of industrial economic activities offers opportunities for industrial geographers to develop appropriate new approaches and tools for analysis. The mandate for geographers to contribute, especially to the industry environment policy debate, is strong and strengthening.

Notes

1. Annual global sulphur production for industrial use is between 55 and 60 million metric tonnes (Ayres et al., 1995). Considerably more sulphur is mobilised, however; for example as a component of coal or as gypsum. Somewhat less than half of that produced for industrial use in 'mine' as elemental sulphur. The remainder is derived in highly reduced form (e.g. as hydrogen sulphide) as a by-product of oil, gas and metals refining. There is only one long lived structural material with a potential economic use that can be safely used to embody waste sulphur (synthetic gypsum i.e., hydrated calcium sulphate), which can be used to make plaster board. In practice, although much waste sulphur from chemical processes ends up combined with calcium (from lime), this is not used for any commercial purpose. It is usually held in ponds. Much of the remaining sulphur becomes combined with sodium during industrial processes, in which case the material, when released into the environment, is soluble and biologically available. A small amount of sulphur is emitted from industrial processes (e.g. wood pulping) in reduced form (hydrogen sulphide and mercaptans). These are toxic.

2. Material and energy are often treated separately. In respect to environmental distubance, however, concern over energy use arises because of the materials mobilisation and transformation implied by combustion, not because of any intrinsic problem with energy release or dissipation per se.

3. This is particularly the case with respect to energy efficiency gains.

4. See, for example, the work of the World Bank's Industrial Pollution Projection Project (Martin et al., 1991; Lucas et al., 1992).

5. It is in this sense that the heavy dependence of our industrial economic system upon oil is of such concern. Perfecting oil production and shipment processes would not solve the environmental problems of oil since these are bound up in the nature of the product itself and in its dissipation through combustion during use.

6. On the negative side of the balance sheet we can count that converters use rare metals such as platinum. These are obtained by mining and refining low grade ores, which is an energy intensive and high-wastage process. Catalytic converter use imposes an added environmental burden since it reduces vehicles fuel efficiency. On the plus side, we

can count a reduction in noxious emissions. However, the reduction may not be as great as originally expected. The effectiveness of converters diminishes with use and age. It is also low in low operating temperatures. Since short trips account for the bulk of vehicles kilometrage, converters may only infrequently operate under optimal conditions.

7.   As indicated earlier, waste sulphur could be made into a gypsum substitute. Possibilities in respect to other waste materials include the use of fly-ash from coal fired utilities as a source material for aluminium and as a substitute for portland cement, and the use of sludge from paper recycling plants as an asbestos substitute. For example of an attempt at materials cycle optimisation within an industrial park, see Cote et al., (1994).

8.   This is a significant limitation, but one which challenges science and society to determine and agree environmental priorities.

9.   Key references describing materials accounting methodology in greater details include BUWAL, 1991; Heijungs, 1992; and SETAC, 1993. For illustrations of applications of materials accounting and LCA methodology the reader is referred to a report produced by the German Ecological Economics Research Institute for the European Commission's Strategic Analysis in Science ad Technology (START) Unit (Start, 1993). This reviews current LCA practice, makes recommendations and identifies research needs. The study reviews 132 public domain LCAs. Software for developing composite process chains, eco-balances and eco-profiles and for performing LCAs are under commercial development. Some are already available (e.g. BMI, TME and NUB, 1993). The European Commission has recently initiated the development of data banks of balanced unit processes for use in the preparation of LCAs.

References

Ayres, R.U. (1988), 'Self organisation in biology and economics', *International Journal on the Unity of the Sciences*, vol. 1, no. 3, also as IIASA Research Report RR-88-1, IIASA, Laxenburg, Austria.

Ayres, R.U. (1994), 'Industrial metabolism: theory and policy'.

Ayres, R.U., Ayres, L., Frankl, P., Lee, H, Wolfgang, N. and Weaver, P.M. (1995), *Materials Cycle Optimisation in the Production of Major Finished Materials*, Report prepared by the Centre for the Management of Environmental Resources of INSEAD for the European Commission DG XII, contract BRE2-CT93-0894, INSEAD, Fontainebleau.

Ayres, R.U., Schlesinger, W.H. and Socolow, R.H. (1994), Human Impacts on the Carbon and Nitrogen Cycles, Chapter in R. Socolow, C. Andrews and F. Berkhout (eds) *Industrial Ecology and Change*, Cambridge Univeristy Press.

Ayres, R.U. and Simonis, U.E. (eds), (1994), *Industrial Metabolism*, United Nations University Press, Tokyo.

Bradley, R. and Richards, D.J. (eds), *The Greening of Industrial Ecosystems*, National Academy Press, Washington DC, pp. 23-37.

Bureau for Environment and Informatics (BMI), The Institute for Applied Environmental Economics (TME) and the Dutch Unilever Companies (NUB) (1993), *Product Improvement Analysis (PIA) User Guide*, TME, The Hague.

Bourgeois, H., Fumat E. and Weaver P.M. (1993), *A Preliminary Input-Output Analysis of Pulp, Paper and Board Products in France*, (unpublished Working Paper), CMER, INSEAD, Fontainebleau.

BUWAL (Swiss Federal Office of Environment, Forests and Landscape) (1991), *Ecobalance of Packaging Materials: State of 1990*, BUWAL, Berne, Switzerland.

Capps C. and Devas H. (1994), *The Impact of Environmental Legislation on the European Paper Industry*, World Paper, Rowe and Maw, London, UK.

Club of Bruxelles (1994), *Environment: New policies of the European Union*, Preparatory Report for the Club of Bruxelles Conference, February, Brussels, Belgium.

Côté, R.P., Ellison R., Grant J., Hall J., Klynstra P., Martin M., Wade P. (1994), *Designing and Operating Industrial Parks as Ecosystems*, School for Resource and Environmental Studies, Faculty of Management, Dalhousie University, Canada.

CSG/Tellus (1992), *CSG/Tellus Packaging Study: Assessing the Impacts of Production and Disposal of Packaging and Public Policy Measures to Alter its Mix*, Reports 1-5, Tellus Institute, Boston.

Frosch, R.A., and Gallopoulos, N.E., (1989), Strategies for Manufacturing,

Scientific American, September 1989, pp. 94-104.

Gabel, H.L. (1990), *Greenpeace versus Ford: Catalytic Converters Come to the UK*, INSEAD Case-Study, INSEAD, Fontainebleau.

Gabel, H.L., (1991), *European Exhaust Emission Standards for Small Cars*, INSEAD Case-Study, INSEAD, Fontainebleau.

Gabel, H.L. (1992), *Industry CFC Replacement Strategies*, INSEAD Case-Study, INSEAD, Fontainebleau.

Galloway, J.N., Thornton, J.D. and Norton, S.A., (1982), 'Trace metals in atmospheric deposition: a review and assessment', *Atmospheric Environment*, vol.. 16, no. 7.

Guinée, J. (1993), *Data for the Normalisation Step within Life Cycle Assessment of Products*, Paper 14, CML (Centre for Environmental Science, Leiden), Leiden, The Netherlands.

Heijungs (ed.) (1992), *Environmental Life Cycle Assessment of Products: Vol I (Guide) and II (Background)*; R. Heijungs (ed.), Report N° 92-66, CML (Centre for Environmental Science, Leiden), The Netherlands.

Jänicke, M., Monch, H., Ranneberg, T. and Simonis, U.E. (1988), *Structural Change and Environmental Impact: Empirical Evidence on Thirty-One Countries in East and West*, Science Centre Berlin, FS 11-88-402, Berlin.

Lohm, U., Anderberg, S. and Bergbäck, B, (1994), 'Industrial metabolism at the national level: a case-study on chromium and lead pollution in Sweden, 1880-1980, in Ayres, Robert, U. and Simonis, U. E. (eds), *Industrial Metabolism: Restructuring for Sustainable Development*, United Nations University Press, Tokyo, pp. 103-118.

Lucas, R., Whe,eler D. and, Hettige H. (1992), *Economic Development, Environmental Regulation and the International Migration of Toxic Industrial Pollution*, World Bank, Washington DC, 1992.

Martin, P., Wheeler, D., Hetttige, M. and Stengen, R. (1991), *The Industrial Pollution Projection System*, World Bank, Washington DC.

National Academy of Sciences (NAS) (1994), *The Greening of Industrial Ecosystems*, National Academy Press, Washington DC.

SAST (Strategic Analysis in Science and Technology, The European Commission) (1993), *Evaluation of Ecobalances*, EUR-14737.

SETAC (Society of Environmental Toxicology and Chemistry) (1993), *Guidelines for Life-Cycle Assessment: A Code of Practice*, Report from the Sesimbra Workshop (March 1993), Sesimbra, Portugal.

Simonis, U.E. (1994), 'Industrial restructuring in industrial countries', in Ayres, R.U. and Simonis, U.E. (eds) *Industrial Metabolism: Restructuring for Sustainable Development*, United Nations University Press, Tokyo, pp. 31-54.

Stigliani, W.M. (1991), *Chemical Time Bombs: Definition, Concepts and Examples*, Executive Report 16, IIASA, Laxenburg, Austria.

Stigliani, W.M. and Jaffe, P.F. (1993), *Industrial Metabolism and River Basin Studies: A New Approach for the Analysis of Chemical Pollution*, IIASA Research Report RR-93-6, IIASA, Laxenburg, Austria.

Udo de Haes, H.A. (1994), *Can All Chains be Closed?*, Inaugural Lecture, Leiden University, Leiden, The Netherlands.

Virtanen, Y. and Nilsson, S. (1992), *Some Environmental Policy Implications of Recycling Paper Products in Western Europe*, IIASA Executive Report 92-22, IIASA, Laxenburg, Austria.

Virtanen, Y. and Nilsson, S. (1993), *Environmental Impacts of Waste Paper Recycling*, Earthscan, London.

Weaver, P.M. (1994a), 'How life-cycle analysis and operational research methods could help clarify environmental policy: the case of fibre recycling in the pulp/paper sector', the paper presented to the IGU Commission Organisation of Industrial Space, Budapest, 16-20 August.

Weaver, P.M. (1994b), *Technological Lock-Out: Threats from Regulatory Environmental Policies in the European Pulpwood, Pulp and Paper Sector*, University of Durham, Durham.

Weaver, P.M., Gabel, H.L., Bloemhof-Ruwaard, J. and Van Wassenhove, L.N. (1995), Environmental Optimisation of the European Pulp and Paper Life Cycle, paper submitted to the 1995 EAERE Conference, Umeå, Sweden.

6 Industrial resource use and transnational conflict: Geographical implications of the James Bay hydropower schemes

Dietrich Soyez

Introduction

Industrial geography has been slow to appreciate issues linked to the environmental impact of industrial activities. While the term 'environment' has been extensively used in the literature of this sub-discipline, the 'natural' or 'ecological' environment has rarely been included. The focus was mostly on specific sectors' or firms' environments - the market, competitors, infrastructure, and institutional actors relevant to industrial corporations. Thus, there is a striking contrast with developments in other related disciplines, such as economics, organisation theory, business administration, and sociology, for example, where environmental issues have been increasingly addressed in recent years (Allenby and Richards, 1994; Beck, 1986; Constanza, 1991; Fischer and Schot, 1993; Hopefenbeck, 1993). It is symptomatic of this problem in industrial geography that the most thorough presentation of the 'industrialisation in the world' that is available in recent German literature addresses the 'environmental problem' only in passing (Voppel, 1990).

It is a major task, and a most important challenge, for industrial geography to fill this gap and to keep up with the rest of geography where the study of environmental issues has a long standing tradition. The purpose of this chapter is to address a specific aspect of an environmentally oriented industrial geography, namely the geographical implications of environmental conflict triggered by industrial resource use.

The focus of the study reported here is neither sectoral nor place-specific. Instead, it tracks the process and progress of conflicts, caused by industrial development in northern Canada, to other regions in North America and Europe. It attempts to map the impact of these conflicts on to both their original locational environment and their most important actors.

One of Canada's largest and most influential corporations, the public utility Hydro-Quebec, is a crucial agent affecting the processes analysed in this study. Not only is it one of the most important actors, it has also triggered environmental conflict. It is claimed, however, that this corporation's economic, political and environmental behaviour, as well as the conflict's evolution and outcome (including the impact on the corporation itself), cannot be understood without a thorough appreciation of what happens in regions far from Quebec - not only in terms of space, but also in terms of cultural, social and mental distance. Thus, the study does not cover a simple spatial or functional domain, such as the corporation itself or its task environment, but cuts across a variety of sectoral, spatial and functional boundaries (for a comparable approach see Soyez, 1981 and 1988). The chapter draws on conceptual ideas and preliminary results from research projects focusing on the international implications of the utilisation of resources in northern Quebec and Newfoundland.[1]

The central topics of these research projects, as well as important aspects of their conceptual approach, are summarised in Figure 6.1 (the 'Goose Bay' military flight training project, however, will not be addressed here.) The basic idea underpinning these studies is that the resource use of industrial societies creates an 'ecological shadow' over their hinterlands (McNeill, Winsemius and Yakushiji, 1991), and that impacted populations try to stop this intrusion by exporting the conflict to transnational arenas.[2] These shadows include the negative impacts of resource extraction and use as well as pollution from distant sources. They are caused by social and cultural conceptions and institutional failures that prevent an adequate assessment and fair distribution of the risks and benefits of economic growth and consumption patterns. The perception of these transnationalisation processes and their impacts are heavily influenced by what Kasperson et al. (1988) have qualified as the 'social amplification of risk' ('SAR' in Figure 6.1), that is quantitative and qualitative disproportions between real and perceived risks. Important results of interest from a spatial point of view are new types of 'social spaces', connected to a variety of categories, such as technology, ethnicity, finance, media or ideologies (in Figure 6.1 these types qualify as 'scapes' according to the terminology proposed by Appadurai (1990).

The concept of the 'ecological shadow' has for the most part been used to characterise existing inequities between the 'North' and the 'South', i.e., between developed and developing nations. In Canada, this north south dichotomy is reversed: the environmental and social costs are borne by economically and socially marginalised groups in the sparsely populated north, while the large majority of Canadians, who live in the south, reap most of the benefits. Comparable north south patterns exist in Norway, Sweden, Japan, and Australia (Dyck, 1991; Jull, 1991).

Both the injection of large scale technologies - with international financing and external end users - and the imposition of outside ideologies, meet with

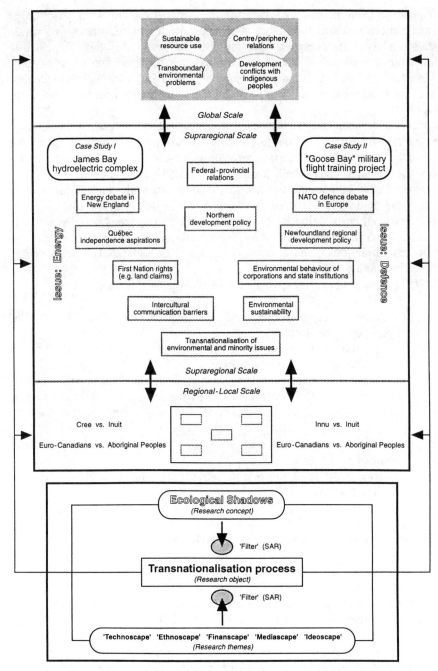

Figure 6.1   Conceptual approach for comparing the James Bay and 'Goose Bay' conflicts

opposition from indigenous peoples in the affected regions. Many no longer expect their concerns to be addressed appropriately within their own nation state, and so, increasingly during the last few years, they have appealed to the international public, the media abroad, and international organisations. These appeals have built on expressions of solidarity, information strategies, and links established in the 1970s among indigenous peoples around the world.

Indigenous peoples have also tried to forge alliances in end user regions at home and abroad. Thus, the catch phrase of sustainable development, 'think globally, act locally' has been reversed, as populations seek outside support for their causes: they 'think locally' but 'act globally' (Barker and Soyez, 1994). These interactions are transnational in nature not only because more than one nation is involved but also because the players often include multinational corporations, international banks, indigenous peoples active in international forums (such as the United Nations organisations) and last, but not least, individuals and grassroots groups with remarkable transboundary behaviour and action spaces.

Within this general framework, the objectives of this chapter are:

• to provide basic background information about the James Bay hydropower projects;
• to map important transnational networks that result from the conflict and influence it at the same time;
• to present results based on two case studies, one from North America, the second from Europe (as well as the linkages between them), in order to promote a better appreciation of both spatial conflict patterns and protagonists' strategies;
• to evaluate repercussions of the conflict from an industrial geographic point of view; and
• to draw some preliminary conclusions as to the conceptual interest of similar studies.

The case study: James Bay Hydroelectric Power Schemes

The government of Quebec and the provincial power utility, Hydro-Quebec (this latter ranking among the five largest electricity producers of the world), are committed to harnessing some 28,000 megawatts of hydroelectric capacity from a number of its northern rivers whose total catchment areas cover almost 400,000 square kilometres. Phase 1, which has harnessed the river La Grande, is nearly completed (on the technical, organisational and environmental background from the proponents' point of view see the extensive documentation provided by Société d' Energie de la Baie James,

110

1987a, b; Hydro-Quebec et al., 1992. Critical appreciations of the projects and their impact are provided by Grand Council of the Crees of Quebec/Cree Regional Authority, 1991; Berkes, 1988; McCutcheon, 1991 and Barber, Orkin and Hazell, 1991). Phase 2, which would place three dams on the Great Whale River, is now undergoing environmental review (see Hydro-Quebec, 1993). A third phase of development, Nottaway-Broadback-Rupert (NBR) is projected for the turn of the century.

The end users, mostly consumers of electricity generated from the power stations, live in southern Quebec, New York, and the New England states. Eventually, Europeans and even Japanese might also become end users if electricity based hydrogen production and liquid hydrogen export (by tanker) prove to be technically feasible and economically sound (Wurster, 1990).

The James Bay project is profoundly modifying the hydrological regime - including water volumes, discharge rates and periodicity, temperature patterns, and ice formation - on some of the large rivers draining the Labrador Ungava peninsula. They also result in substantial changes for the inland waters and coastal region, although quantitative data are rare and prognoses difficult. From an ecological point of view, in particular, the river diversions must be considered some of the most radical modifications of the natural environment. One of the more spectacular diversions is that of River Caniapiscau, as a substantial part of its upstream water is now flowing west into James Bay instead of north into Ungava Bay. One of the most radical diversions is that of River Eastmain which now, compared to natural conditions, runs almost dry with down to just one tenth of its original discharge.

Although the scale of the project makes impact prediction and evaluation difficult, substantial habitat loss as well as changes in habitat and wildlife populations are already evident, especially in highly biologically productive wetland areas. The accumulation of methyl mercury in the large reservoirs, produced by anaerobic decomposition concentration in food chains, constitute critical problems, in particular as inland water fish constitutes an important part of indigenous peoples' normal diet.

Impacts seen by project proponents as controllable or capable of mitigation are viewed by opponents as irreversible and existence threatening. The affected peoples are mostly Cree Indians and Inuit living on the northern fringe of the project area. Some 4,700 aboriginal people live in two Cree and four Inuit communities located within the area of the Great Whale project alone.

In response to a Cree court[3] challenge aimed at halting Phase 1, the Quebec government negotiated a treaty with the Cree and Inuit in 1975 - the *James Bay and Northern Quebec Agreement*. Confronted with Phase 2 and later possibly a third phase of development, the Cree are now challenging the provisions of the 1975 agreement. Key actors in the current dispute include

111

Hydro-Quebec, the government of Quebec, local and international corporations (in particular aluminium and magnesium consortia), the Grand Council of the Cree, public utilities in New York and some New England states, environmental and human rights groups in Canada and in the United States and, to a lesser extent, in Europe. The conflict has been played out before the courts, in state energy and environmental hearings in the northeastern United States, just to mention a few arenas, and events such as press conferences, workshops, rallies and happenings of the most diverse nature organised by project opponents, have abounded (particularly between 1991 and 1993). There is also a clear interdependence with the heated constitutional dispute between French speaking Quebecois and the rest of Canada.

Transnational implications of the hydropower schemes and the ensuing conflict

A number of the transnational implications and conflicts of the James Bay hydropower schemes have already been mentioned and these will be explored in greater detail in this section. These transnational implications are apparent as much for the projects' proponents as for their opponents. They embrace the international financing, technical and public relations activity of Hydro-Quebec, international energy markets and the international lobbying of governments, authorities, institutions, media and researchers.

Both the scale and the scope of the James Bay projects would have been impossible without heavy reliance on external sources of finance, technology and public relations. The construction of Phase 1 would have been impossible without tapping into U.S. and European (in particular German) capital markets. Indeed, between 1969 and 1991, an amount of DM 3.32 billion was raised in Germany alone (Drouin, 1991). Also for specific technical aspects of the projects, most notably high voltage transmission and turbine construction, Hydro-Quebec was dependent on foreign expertise and foreign corporations. This was particularly the case in the start-up phase of the project although today, Hydro-Quebec and Quebec engineering firms are considered to rank among the world's experts in these fields. Finally, the difficult challenge of responding to what was considered, in Quebec, as an international 'smear' and 'disinformation' campaign orchestrated by the Cree Indians and their allies (see below) made it necessary, in the opinion of Quebec's most influential decision-makers, to enlist the services of the world's best known and controversial public relations firm, Burson-Marsteller.

Without the prospect of selling the electricity abroad, especially to customers in New England and New York, neither the scope nor the scale of the planned hydropower schemes would have made sense. Consequently, there was a clear strategy to sign contracts with as many utilities south of the Canadian border, in particular with those linked to large New York and New England utilities (The New York Power Authority and NEPOOL). The apparent strategy was to use sales to the American market to pay the heavy debt burden during the difficult first or second decades of the projects, with the domestic Canadian market then being able to take advantage of the capacities which by then would have been paid for through sales to the Americans.

During the late 1980s, however, a new promising market seemed to develop in Europe, particularly in Germany - the hydrogen market. Increasing pollution levels and environmental damage in Europe had prepared the base for research on a future hydrogen 'path', mostly, but not exclusively, to power cars (Gretz et al., 1989, Wurster, 1990). Hydrogen was considered, by all the Europeans involved - politicians as well as researchers - as 'clean energy', especially if it was produced by hydroelectricity. This was the background for the massive funding, by the European Union, the Government of Quebec and influential European industrial corporations, of the EQHHPP ("Euro-Quebec Hydro-Hydrogen Pilot-Project"), with the aim of completing a feasibility study during the early 1990s. This project linked together the cream of, in particular, German corporations and research institutions. The EQHHPP was based on a very modest 100 MW share of Quebec's hydroelectric capacity, but the idea was, of course, to dedicate considerably more capacity to this market once demand increased in Europe.

However these corporate, technical and marketing developments excited an international lobbying response involving governments, authorities, institutions, media and researchers. It took some time for corporate and government decision makers in Quebec to realise the potential threat posed by the project's opponents. Hydro-Quebec versus a handful of Cree Indians and their supporters seemed almost ridiculous. On one side was the energy producer with its huge manpower in the most diverse fields and immense financial and legal resources. On the other side were the local Indians, supported by a few Euro-Canadian and American advisers, almost devoid of financial, political and legal power in the Canadian domestic context.

However, the Crees' campaign against the James Bay projects gained considerable speed and clout once they started to target existing and potential buyers of Quebec electricity in the New England states and New York. In this campaign they were supported by local and regional American groups with the most diverse background, strategies and intentions.

In order to counter the seemingly disastrous effect their opponents' campaign in the media and among the general public in the US and in Europe made every possible effort to lobby local and regional governments, state assemblies, utilities, and the media, especially in the United States. Hydro-

Quebec set up an office in Brussels (in September, 1991), headed by a Vice-president, to better control the situation in Europe (with regard to the media and governments). An office was re-opened in New York in 1992 with a permanent representative. Wherever project opponents made their appearance around the world, be it at universities, conferences or other meetings and events of high visibility, Quebec corporate or government officials tried to contain the impact of non-official viewpoints (for example at the Olympic Games in Barcelona in 1992, and at the so-called International Water Tribunal in Amsterdam in 1992). The attempt to assess the risk potential of European environmental and human rights groups supporting the Cree efforts to stop Phase 2 ('Great Whale') of the project is clearly documented in the confidential study of Burson-Marsteller (France) commissioned by Hydro-Quebec.

From this discussion a strong conclusion can be drawn. From being an only regionally important player until the early 1970s, Hydro-Quebec had become, in the early 1990s, a transnational actor, diligently supported by Quebec's extensive (being a 'province' of a federal state) network of diplomatic representations all over the world through 'Trade Representatives', 'Delegations', 'Delegations Générales'). Thus, the conflict around James bay intensified considerably a transnationalisation trend that had existed, almost unnoticed, since the early 1970s.

This evolution of Hydro-Quebec is mirrored, but with a time lag of almost two decades, by a similar transnationalisation of indigenous behaviour. Early academic appreciation of this trend is found in Woodward and George (1983), Jhappan (1990) and Pointing (1990). The fact of this development is even more astonishing since the Cree Indians had lived, up until the early 1970s, in rather isolated bands or small communities, with almost no continuous contact with southern Canada.

Whereas the conflict around Phase 1 of the James Bay schemes virtually 'parachuted' at least some of the Cree leaders into the Euro-Canadian world (for example, the then Chief, Billy Diamond) (see McGregor, 1990), the pervasive transnational did not start before the announcement, by Hydro-Quebec, of Phase 2 ('Great Whale') at the end of the 1980s. Feeling almost helpless in the domestic arena compared to the resources of the project proponents, the Cree started, supported by a number of Euro-Canadian advisers (anthropologists, legal experts and energy experts), to defend their cause in some New England communities, contacting directly Hydro-Quebec's US customers. Surprised by the positive response, they intensified this approach, and very soon their efforts were paralleled by the similar activities of more than a dozen very active (and hundreds of affiliated) environmental and human rights groups in the whole of northeastern US (Barden, 1994).

The activities of these groups included academic and non-academic lectures, artistic performances, happenings, rallies, media work, phone campaigns to inform and to prompt local and regional MPs and politicians (both with and without Cree participation). At the same time, and already much more consciously, links were established with other indigenous organisations both in North America and worldwide. This interlinking was facilitated by the fact that the Grand Council of the Crees (of Quebec) had been awarded, by the United Nations, official NGO (non-government organisation) status in the late 1980s, enabling the Cree leaders to defend their cause in UN commissions. Before long, Cree representatives were invited to appear and to speak in the most diverse contexts all over the world. Nowadays, the Cree themselves choose events of high visibility in order to proceed with what Canadian anthropologists have termed the 'politics of embarrassment', both in the domestic and in international arenas.[4]

To sum up, within less than half a decade Cree representatives have become global actors, under intense conflict pressure and with the support of allies in many countries, trying to stop Phase 2 of the James Bay project at home by forging international links and exerting pressure anywhere in the world, not only on Quebec but also on any Canadian corporate and government representative who happen to defend the project.

It goes without saying that the disputes between the antagonists has sometimes turned quite ugly, an aspect that will not be analysed here.[5]

The transnational activities of all the parties, together with their internal and external linkages, offers insight into past and present conflict patterns. However, in order to understand these patterns of conflict and the interactions they have involved requires a greater amount of empirical data. The approach used in the present research is that of mapping the existing networks and relationships and, as far as this is possible, identifying the types and the intensities of interactions.

Transnational networks and the James Bay projects

Because limitations of space deny the possibility of going into greater detail, it must be mentioned at the outset that the James Bay related networks have been studied in-depth mainly in the northeastern USA[6] and in Germany. A summary of the findings of these studies is presented in Figures 6.2 to 6.5. Figure 6.2 is a graph showing how Figures 6.3 to 6.5 relate to each other. The specific framework of enquiry designed for this research is a set of 'Chinese Boxes' where the various shells represent various scales from local to continental and global (Figure 6.3 and 6.4). 'Unofficial' actors (in particular interest and pressure groups) are plotted into the lower half of the graph. 'Official' actors, such as governments and authorities are plotted into the upper half. The linkages shown are well documented by empirical data.

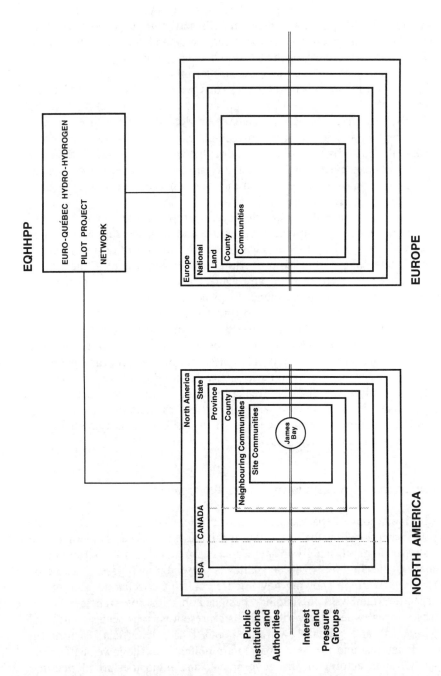

EQHHPP

EURO-QUÉBEC HYDRO-HYDROGEN

PILOT PROJECT

NETWORK

Europe
National
Land
County
Communities

EUROPE

North America
State
Province
County
Neighbouring Communities
Site Communities

USA | CANADA

James Bay

NORTH AMERICA

Public
Institutions
and
Authorities

Interest
and
Pressure
Groups

Figure 6.2   James Bay: North American-European linkages

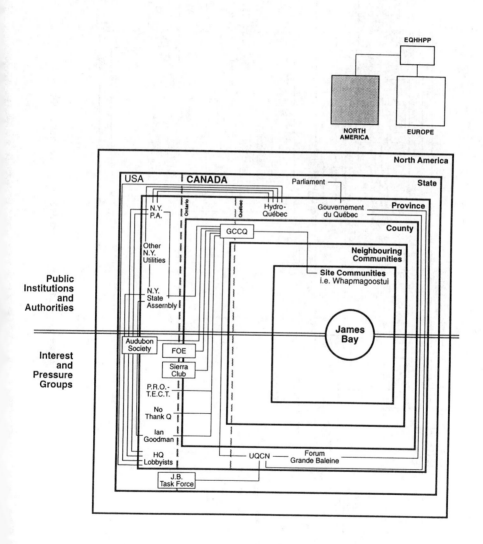

Figure 6.3   Important actors as to the James Bay issue in North America (selected)

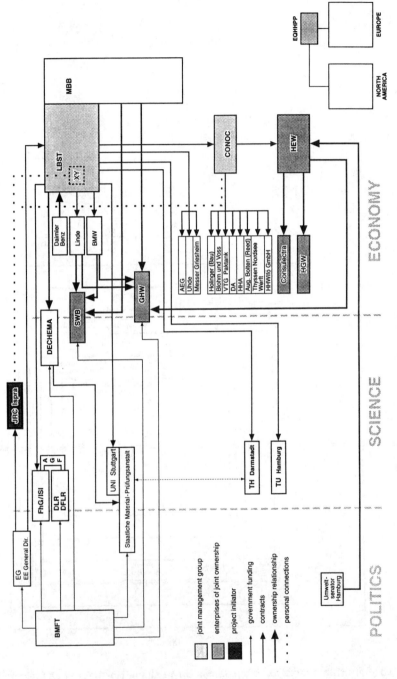

Figure 6.4   EQHHPP - related network in Germany (Phase II)

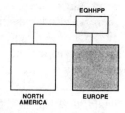

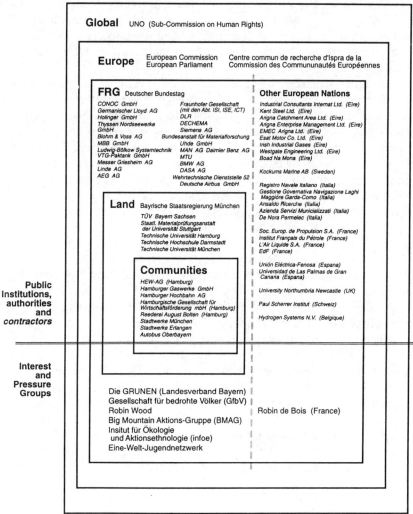

EQHHPP

NORTH AMERICA   EUROPE

Global UNO (Sub-Commission on Human Rights)

Europe European Commission   Centre commun de recherche d'Ispra de la
European Parliament   Commission des Commununautés Européennes

FRG Deutscher Bundestag

CONOC GmbH	Fraunhofer Gesellschaft
Germanischer Lloyd AG	(mit den Abt. ISI, ISE, ICT)
Holinger GmbH	DLR
Thyssen Nordseewerke	DECHEMA
GmbH	Siemens AG
Blohm & Voss AG	Bundesanstalt für Materialforschung
MBB GmbH	Uhde GmbH
Ludwig-Bölkow Systemtechnik	MAN AG Daimler Benz AG
VTG-Paktank GmbH	MTU
Messer Griesheim AG	BMW AG
Linde AG	DASA AG
AEG AG	Wehrtechnische Dienststelle 52
	Deutsche Airbus GmbH

Other European Nations

Industrial Consultants Internat Ltd. (Eire)
Kent Steel Ltd. (Eire)
Arigna Catchment Area Ltd. (Eire)
Arigna Enterprise Management Ltd. (Eire)
EMEC Arigna Ltd. (Eire)
Esat Motor Co. Ltd. (Eire)
Insh Industrial Gases (Eire)
Westgate Engineering Ltd. (Eire)
Boad Na Mona (Eire)

Kockums Marine AB (Sweden)

Registro Navale Italiano (Italia)
Gestione Governativa Navigazione Laghi
 Maggiòre Garda-Como (Italia)
Ansaldo Ricerche (Italia)
Azienda Servizi Municializzati (Italia)
De Nora Permelec (Italia)

Soc. Europ. de Propulsion S.A. (France)
Institut Français du Pétrole (France)
L'Air Liquide S.A. (France)
EdF (France)

Unión Eléctrica-Fenosa (Espana)
Universidad de Las Palmas de Gran
 Canaria (Espana)

University Northumbria Newcastle (UK)

Paul Scherrer Institut (Schweiz)

Hydrogen Systems N.V. (Belgique)

Land Bayrische Staatsregierung München

TÜV Bayern Sachsen
Staatl. Materialprüfungsanstalt
 der Universität Stuttgart
Technische Universität Hamburg
Technische Hochschule Darmstadt
Technische Universität München

Communities

HEW-AG (Hamburg)
Hamburger Gaswerke GmbH
Hamburger Hochbahn AG
Hamburgische Gesellschaft für
 Wirtschaftsförderung mbH (Hamburg)
Reederei August Bolten (Hamburg)
Stadtwerke München
Stadtwerke Erlangen
Autobus Oberbayern

Public Institutions, authorities and contractors

Interest and Pressure Groups

Die GRUNEN (Landesverband Bayern)
Gesellschaft für bedrohte Völker (GfbV)
Robin Wood
Big Mountain Aktions-Gruppe (BMAG)
Insitut für Ökologie
 und Aktionsethnologie (infoe)
Eine-Welt-Jugendnetzwerk

Robin de Bois (France)

Figure 6.5   Important actors as to the James Bay issue in Europe (Phase III.)
(EQHHPP actors in italics, c.f. figure 6.4)

Also, Figure 6.5, which is a more detailed presentation of the Federal Republic of Germany part of Figure 6.4, shows a network structure, but the actors here are not 'spatially rooted' in the sense that they represent economic, political or environmental interest of a specific region. On the contrary, most actors of the Euro-Quebec Hydro-Hydrogen Pilot-Project (EQHHPP) network are 'footloose'. It is more or less accidental where they are located.

The mapping of these networks is not an aim in itself. They are used to ask questions, to form hypotheses and to better understand some of the mechanisms typical of all networks, such as: which are the flows of information, pressure, money, perceptions or ideologies; where is the power; where are barriers, nodes or gatekeepers; and what gradients exist? (Wellman, 1988)

Three examples illustrate the consequences of specific network linkages between Quebec and Germany. First, consider two very different opinions in these countries as to environmental problems. No matter how large the differences are, insofar these two worlds are not linked to each other, nothing will happen. Once they are linked, the situation changes dramatically: There will be gradients, and along these gradients, information, values, perceptions and pressure (just to mention a few possible categories) will start to flow and to influence each other, despite the fact that an ocean divides Quebec and Germany. If most Germans think that the environmental and social costs of large hydroelectric projects are unacceptably high while Quebeckers think that these externalities can be mitigated, then Quebec would run into problems if it tried to sell hydroelectric products, such as hydrogen, in Germany.

The conclusion is clear, every protagonist (James Bay proponent or opponent), has to identify appropriate channels as well as the most important nodes of economic, legal, and political power, both domestically and internationally. Then the 'right' information (or attitude or perception) must be channelled to the appropriate target group or institution. The protagonists on both sides will simultaneously try to hamper each other, or, if they lack the power to do so directly, they will try to counteract their opponents by channelling their own version to the same or other influential targets. The overall goal is to get one's message across and to neutralise the opponent's message. Individuals can play a crucial role by identifying and occupying strategic points in channels and nodes: they serve as gatekeepers, influencing the nature and flow of information. This adds a highly political dimension to normal entrepreneurial procedures of industrial decision making and impact.

Second, there is the issue of control or attempted control of the flow of information within networks, an issue that holds considerable consequences from an industrial geographic point of view. In order to keep competitive advantage and to avoid problems with domestic customers, the Quebec

120

government concluded confidential power contracts, offering very advantageous tariffs, with several multinational aluminium consortia (including 'Alouette' to which Germany's most important aluminium corporation belongs). The content of one of these contracts, concluded with the Norwegian corporation Norsk Hydro, was leaked in early 1991 in Norway and Australia, but not in Canada. Its publication in Quebec was stopped at the request of the government by a court injunction. However, this attempt at information flow control did not work, not only because the information was already published outside Quebec, but because a cable TV station based in Burlington, VT, channelled it to its customers in Montreal. The publication of this information resulted in a comparable blocking action in another field. A US competitor complained, within the framework of the North American Free Trade Agreement (NAFTA), about unfair subsidies awarded by the Quebec government to its domestic magnesium producers and raised accusations of dumping. Eventually, a high additional tax charge was imposed on magnesium exported from Canada to the United States, thus partly neutralising the locational and tariff advantages of smelters in Quebec (although, as it later turned out, only temporarily).

Third, there are issues surrounding the consequences of the control of information by gatekeepers. These consequences can be shown in the network linking the German EQHHPP network (shown in Figure 6.5) with Canada. Due to the fact that German researchers' connections were for a long time restricted to the only official Quebecois decision makers, they were not informed appropriately about the environmental and social consequences of hydroelectricity production at James Bay. Their Quebecois counterparts were not very outspoken either about the ongoing conflicts between Hydro-Quebec and the Cree Indians. Only recently have the German EQHHPP partners realised how questionable it is, at least from an European viewpoint, to qualify hydrogen produced in Quebec as 'clean'. Thus, the German researchers fell victims of a significant loss of scientific and ethical credibility due to this 'lack of information' caused by foreign gatekeepers.

Geographical implications

The geographical implications of the network analyses outlined in this chapter are many and varied. The principal focus of the present study has been on those impacts that can be linked directly or indirectly to the conflicts over the James Bay hydropower projects played out around the world.

The direct impacts involve in a very real sense, structural changes in spatial systems of interactions and interrelationships and three broad types can be identified. First, there has been project modification in response to pressure. There have been engineering changes with regard to original plans, for example, redesign of dams and reservoirs and relocation of power houses. Also mitigation measures have been adopted to ameliorate environmental and infrastructure impacts, for example. The most radical direct impacts have been 'non-events'; when, for instance, project proponents have not proceeded as originally planned, and have left a catchment area intact or have not proceeded with a planned river diversion.

Second, power supply systems, in Quebec and elsewhere have been modified. Increased emphasis has been placed on energy conservation, the modification of traditional power generation mixes and, most radical of all, the consistent adoption of 'demand side management, and least cost planning' strategies by the power utilities. The most dramatic event of this kind did not happen in Canada but in New York. In part due to conflict pressure, the New York Power Authority cancelled a multi billion dollar contract with Hydro-Quebec in early 1992, thus seriously jeopardising the whole of Phase 2 of the James Bay project. A similar direct impact was the postponement of the Great Whale scheme and the eventual acceptance of the Quebec government to proceed with an independent environmental review.

Third, there have been strategy changes in the environmental behaviour of governments, institutions, individuals and utilities, thus laying the ground for long term changes in environmental impacts. Indeed, incremental changes can be detected in the behaviour of Hydro-Quebec, in particular in relation to energy conservation.

More indirect impacts are, for example, changes in the locational behaviour of electricity consuming industries in Quebec or changes in consumer behaviour due to long term prospects for energy tariffs of the availability of electricity.

A completely different, but nonetheless extremely important, geographical implication of these environmental conflicts is what has been described as 'network extension'; the extension of the action and activity spaces of all the protagonists involved in the conflicts. It goes without saying that these extensions are paralleled (and also partly prepared) by completely modified spatial perceptions. The 'gradients' of information and inequality that characterise those extended networks, as well as the actors involved (whether they are gatekeepers or not), can trigger directly or indirectly, spatial impacts in regions far away. Thus, from a geographical point of view network relationships affect globalisation processes, including their homogenising and heterogenising effects, and that tendency to increase either consensus or conflict. Finally it should be emphasised that all the impacts discussed here create completely new types of not only 'social space' but also other types of 'space' that are increasingly the subject of theoretical geography and other social sciences (see for example Appadurai, 1990; and Barker and Soyez, 1994).

122

Conclusions

Large scale industrial resource use in industrialised countries' hinterlands cast 'ecological shadows' producing a variety of detrimental effects on politically and socially marginalised populations - far away from the end users regions where most of the development's benefits are reaped. As the impacted populations do not feel themselves in a position to defend their cause appropriately in the domestic arena, they try to transnationalise the conflict by forging alliances with supporters in the end user regions (and elsewhere) in order to put pressure on the development's proponents. This can lead to the significant modification of original plans (the most radical effect being their complete abandonment) with ensuing effects on industrial and other spatial systems. Conflict pressure will also affect, and eventually modify, the environmental behaviour of corporations, governments, institutions and individuals, thus laying the ground for changed (and hopefully reduced) environmental effects in the future.

Transnational conflict and interaction patterns of the sort outlined in this chapter are changing the face of the world, and networks of the type described here are the agent transmitting change. They should help us to reappraise not only the character and the scope of ongoing globalisation processes, but also the traditional view of core-periphery relationships and the shaping of new types of relevant 'spaces'. Understanding network relationships, the 'spaces' they create and their impacts on corporations, industrial sectors and industrial landscapes, is an important task for industrial and economic geography, as it focuses on industry-environment interrelationships and interactions.

Acknowledgements

The generous financial support of Deutsche Forschungsgemeinschaft (Bonn/Germany) and the European Communities, DG XII-Area 3 (Brussels/Belgium) is gratefully acknowledged. Mary L. Barker and H. Peter Dörrenbächer provided most valuable help both from a conceptual and a practical point of view. They deserve heartfelt thanks for their cooperation.

Notes

1. The titles of the research projects are:
   (1)'Periphere Ressourcennutzung and Trandnationalisierungsprozesse, dargestellt and Beispielen aus Quebec und Neu-Fundland, Kanada' (grant So 108/8-1 by Deutsche Forschungsgemeinschaft, Bonn) (jointly conducted with Mary L. Barker, Karlsruhe), and,
   (2) a sub project of 'landscape and Life: Appropriate Scales for Sustainable Development' (grant EV5B-CT92-0138 by DG XII-Area 3, European Communities, Brussels, Coordinator: Anne Buttimer, University College Dublin, Ireland) (jointly conducted with H. Peter Dörrenbächer, Universität des Saarlandes, Saarbrücken.

2. 'Economic activity today is concentrated in the world's urban/industrial regions. Few, if any, of these regions are ecologically self-contained. They breathe, drink, feed, and work on the ecological capital of their 'hinterland', which also receives their accumulated wastes [...]. This ecological capital, which may be found thousands of miles from the regions in which it is used, forms the 'shadow ecology' of an economy'. (McNeill, Winsemius and Yakushiji, 1991, pp. 58-59)

3. A court injunction, unique in Canadian Aboriginal disputes, led to a complete stop of all construction work for several days (Malouf, 1993) but was listed by Quebec's Supreme Court, basically stating that some thousand indians could not stop what was important to several million Quebecois.

4. An illustrative example of the approach adopted by the Cree is the written statement submitted by the Grand Council of the Crees (of Quebec) entitled 'Discrimination against indigenous populations', August 22, 1988 (UN Economic and Social Council, 1988).

5. See, for example, project opponents' one page advertisement in the New York Times of October 21, 1991 (comparing the James Bay project to the destruction of the Amazon region) and the ensuing disputes in the US and Canadian media.

6. This is the objective of a master's thesis ('Diplomarbeit'), conducted within and financed by the research project, to map as exactly as possible the network formed by supportive US groups in New England and New York. (see Barden, 1994). The help of grassroots groups and individuals is gratefully acknowledged, especially Professor Floyd Henderson (Department of Geography, SUNY, Albany and his wife.

References

Appadurai, A. (1990), 'Disjuncture and difference in the global cultural economy', in Featherstone, M. (ed.), *Global Culture: Nationalism, Globalization and Modernity,* Sage, London, pp. 295-310.

Allenby, B.R. and Richards, D.J. (eds), (1994), *The Greening of Industrial Ecosystems,* National Academy of Engineering, Oxford.

Barber, M., Orkin, A. and Hazell, S. (1991), *The Three Gorges Dam Project, China ("Three Gorges") and the James Bay Hydroelectric Project, Quebec, Canada ("James Bay"),* unpublished paper, Toronto/Ottawa.

Barden, S. (1994) 'James Bay - related transboundary conflict: information diffusion and environmental networking in the northeastern USA', *Ahornblätter (Marburger Beiträge zur Kanada-Forschung),* vol. 7, pp. 98-115.

Barker, M.L. and Soyez, D. (1994), 'Think locally - act globally? the transnationalisation of Canadian resource - use conflicts', *Environment,* vol. 36, no. 5, pp. 12-20, 32-36.

Beck, U. (1986), *Die Risikogesellschaft,* Suhrkamp, Frankfurt a.M.

Berkes, F. (1988) 'The intrinsic difficulty of predicting impacts: lessons from the James Bay Hydro Project', *Environmental Impact Assessment Review,* no. 8, pp. 201-220.

Constanza, R. (ed.) (1991), *Ecological Economics. The Science and management of Sustainability,* Columbia University Press, New York.

Drouin, R. (1991), Paper presented at Deutsch-Kanadischer Wirtschaftsklub, Köln, November 19.

Dyck, N. (ed.) (1991), *Indigenous People and the Nation-State: 'FourthWorld' Politics in Canada, Australia and Norway,* Institute of Social and Economic Research, Social and Economic Studies, University of Newfoundland, St. John's.

Fischer, K. and Schot, J. (eds) (1993), *Environmental Strategies for Industry, International Perspectives on research Needs and Policy Implications,* Island Press, Washington DC and Covel, CA.

Grand Council of the Crees (of Quebec), Cree Regional Authority (1991), *Environmental-Economic and Social Issues Related to the James Bay Phase II Project,* unpublished paper, Ottawa.

Graze, J., Baselt, J.P., Ullman, O. and Wendt, H. (1989), *The 100MW Euro-Quebec Hydro-Hydrogen Pilot Project,* VDI-Berichte.

Hopfenbeck, W. (1993), *Umweltorientiertes Management und Marketing,* Verlag Moderne Industrie.

Hydro-Quebec (1992), *James Bay and Northern Quebec Hydroelectric Development,* unpublished paper presented to Second International Water Tribunal, Amsterdam, February 17-21.

125

Hydro-Quebec (1993), *Grande Baleine Complex. Feasibility Study (Summary)*, Montreal.

Jhappan, C.R. (1990), 'Indian symbolic politics: the double-edged sword of publicity', *Canadian Ethnic Studies,* vol. 22, no. 3, pp. 19-39.

Jull, P. (1991), *The Politics of Northern Frontiers in Australia, Canada and other 'First World' Countries,* Australian National University, Casuarina NT.

Kasperson, R.E., Renn, O., Slovic, P., Brown, H.S., Emel, J. R. Goble, J.X. Kasperson and Ratick, S. (1988), 'The social amplification of risk: a conceptual framework', *Risk Analysis,* vol.8, no.2, pp. 177-187.

MacNeill, J. Winsemius, J.P. and Yakushiji, T. (1991), *Beyond Interdependence: the Meshing of the World's economy and the Earth's Ecology,* Oxford University Press, New York.

Malouf, A. (1993), *La baie James indienne,* Édition du Jour, Montreal.

MsCutcheon, S. (1991), *Electric Rivers,* Montreal: Black Rose, Montreal.

McGregor, R. (1991), *Chief,* Penguin, Harmondsworth.

Ponting, J.R. (1990), 'Internationalization: perspectives on an emerging direction in aboriginal affairs', *Canadian Ethnic Studies,* XXII, vol. 22, no. 3, pp. 85-109.

Société d'Energie de la Baie James (1987a), *Le complexe hydroélectrique de La Grande Rivière. Réalisation de la première phase,* Montreal.

Société d'Energie de la Baie James (1987b), *Le défie environnement au complexe hydroélectrique de La grand Rivière,* Montreal.

Soyez, D. (1988), 'Scandinavian siliculture in Canada: entry and performance barriers', *The Canadian Geographer,* vol. 32, no. 2, pp. 133-140.

United Nations, Economic and Social Council (1988), *Discriminating against indigenous populations* (Written Statement submitted by Grand Council of the Crees (of Quebec), a non-governmental organisation on the Roster), E/CN.4/Sub. 2/1988/NGO/20, 22 August 1988.

Voppel, G. (1990), *Die Industrialisierung der Erde,* Teubner, Stuttgart.

Wellman, B. (1988), 'Structural analysis: from method and metaphor to theory and substance', in Wellman, B. and Berkowitz, S.D. (eds) *Social structures: a network approach,* Cambridge University Press, Cambridge, pp. 19-61.

Woodward, M. and George, B. (1983), 'The Canadian Indian lobby of Westminster: 1978-1982', *Journal of Canadian Studies,* vol. 18, no. 3.

Wurster, R. (1990), 'Die nordischen Energiereserven aus Wasserkraft in Kanada, Island, Grönland, und ihre Nutzung, dargestellt am Beispiel des Euro-Quebec Hydro-Hydrogen Pilot Projects', *Umweltverträgliche Energieversorgung, 2. Int. CMDC Jahreskongress,* Zurich, pp. 294-306.

Part II: The state, policy and the environment

The role of the state in sanctioning, moulding and manipulating environment-economy interrelationships through the formulation of policy and regulation is the subject of the chapters in Part II. Ooi highlights the importance of environmental policy and its enforcement in establishing environment-economy relationships in the rapidly industrialising countries of East and Southeast Asia and focuses analysis on the situation in Singapore. In Singapore, policy has been orientated towards the control of pollution rather than the protection and management of the environment. Thus, nature conservation has been neglected and public participation in setting an environmental agenda has been compromised by the strong role of the state and the emphasis that has been given to developmentalist economic policies.

Gibbs and Healey address the role of local government in formulating strategies for the sustainable management of the local environment. In the context of local government in the UK, they outline the progress that has been made in developing local policy approaches. However, they show clearly that approaching sustainable development from the purely local level is not enough. There is a tension between 'policies from above' (in relation to both national and European Union policies in the case of the UK) and 'policies from below' (such as the formulation of local pollution controls). They also suggest that market mechanisms are not enough to stimulate change in the way the environment is used and that legislative and policy frameworks are equally important to achieving such change.

Singh, Pandey and Singh explore the relationships between economic development and the environment in the developing country of India context through a detailed study of the Ram Nagar Industrial Estate in Uttar Pradesh. They demonstrate not only the success of economic development but also the environmental threats that development poses. Those threat arise in part from the process of economic growth but are intensified by a lack of information, the uneven enforcement of environmental standards, inadequate training on environmental issues and political interference and corruption in environmental management.

7 Environmental management in Singapore

Ooi Giok-Ling

Introduction

Economic growth in Southeast Asia's rapidly industrialising countries has tended in the past to focus more on its pace than on its environmental impacts. The benefits to GDP, employment and trade have received far more attention than the environmental costs that have been incurred. The purpose of this chapter is to examine the process of industrialisation in Singapore, its impact on the physical environment, and the strategies that have been introduced to cope with that impact. A key concern of the discussion is the central role that the state has played and continues to play in industrialisation, and the formulation of policy to address its environmental impacts.

The aim of the discussion is not to argue for strong state intervention in environmental protection but rather to highlight the importance of environmental policy and its effective enforcement in rapidly industrialising economies. In the absence of strong grassroots and non-government movements such as the green bans in Australia (Kilmartin et al., 1985), it is the state's policy framework which provides the guidelines for environmental management in Singapore. The areas that have been neglected by this policy framework have in recent years, seen the emergence of stronger non-government organisation activity, particularly in support of nature conservation.

In highlighting the environmental costs of industrialisation in some East and Southeast Asian countries, it is evident that there is a major difference among these newly industrialising economies. This difference has been the importance attached to the need for environmental protection and management because of the rapid pace of industrialisation. In a feature on economic development and the environment in newly industrialising countries in East Asia, including Taiwan, South Korea, Hong Kong and Singapore, it was highlighted that Taiwan's limit on emissions of sulphur dioxide by factories is 750 parts per million, five times the limit applied in Los Angeles and, until recently, South Korea and Hong Kong were reportedly not much better (*The Economist*, November 16th, 1991, p. 19; Newman, 1994). Apart from the problem of traffic congestion, air and water pollution in the large metropolitan centre of Bangkok in Thailand reflect some of the environmental problems being experienced in Asia's booming economies and rapidly growing cities.

Outside the cities, problems of soil degradation and floods have been blamed on deforestation in several Southeast Asian countries like the Philippines. Equally of concern to environmentalists and the people in the region are massive forest fires reported in Indonesia which have been occurring at relatively frequent intervals of some three to four years (Samah, 1994). Such fires not only contribute to deforestation and the destruction of pristine rain and peat forests but also cause considerable air pollution because of the haze spreading to the neighbouring countries of Singapore and parts of Malaysia. These forest fires, like other evidence of environmental degradation, point in the direction of economies where growth is emphasised over environmental protection, with resources allocated accordingly.

Environmental management concerns have, of course, been incorporated into the agenda for regional cooperation among member states of the Association of Southeast Asian Nations' (ASEAN) since 1981.[1] Until recently, this regional association has been more preoccupied with regional security. Lately, however, more emphasis has been given to economic cooperation, trade and the environment.

Interregional comparison of levels of environmental pollution, particularly air and water pollution, is made difficult because of the different indicators that are used and the different methods of measurement that are employed from one country to another. Notwithstanding these problems, available data suggest that environmental problems, such as air pollution, are escalating alarmingly.

Despite the difficulty of drawing comparisons between countries, there are areas of common concern in a number of rapidly industrialising countries in Asia. Management of one such area, river and river basin pollution, has been the focus of environmental work in several East and Southeast Asian countries. Given the varying priority that has been allocated to environmental work, it is not surprising that there has been only limited success in the cleaning up of major rivers and river basins in the region as the following discussion well illustrates.

The environmental crisis in rapidly industrialising Asian countries

Industrialisation in Asia has had a wide range of environmental impacts including those that have affected air quality. In the city state of Singapore, 'an intensive industrialisation programme at the start of the 1960s represents the first major policy to affect the physical environment' (Wong, 1989, p. 777; Lee, 1973, p. 31 and p. 54). If manufacturing industry's share of GDP is used as a measure of the level of industrialisation, then the other rapidly industrialising economies in Southeast Asia are fast reaching the level that has been achieved in Singapore (see Table 7.1). Similarly, the share of the labour force in the manufacturing and service sectors has grown by leaps and bounds in the countries of Asia and Southeast Asia. In 1992, the proportion in Malaysia was 74 per cent compared to 42 per cent in 1965. The proportion in Indonesia in 1992 was 44 per cent, 55 per cent in the Philippines, 100 per cent in Singapore and 33 per cent in Thailand (UNDP Human Development Report, 1994).

Table 7.1
Share of manufacturing in gross domestic product

Country	1985 (per cent)	1990* (per cent)
Thailand	22.1	26.1
Malaysia	17.9	25.1
Singapore	23.6	29.6
Indonesia	14.4	19.4
Philippines	24.6	24.7**

*   Estimates
**   1989

Source: B. Nijathaworn and D. Vongpradhip, 1993, p.3

The toll, in environmental terms, that such rapid industrialisation has exacted, is evident in both the cities and the countryside of Asia. Proof of the ecological crisis created by decades of excessive pollution can be found in the rivers and river basins in Asia. Recognition of the urgent need to clean up and address the environmental damage is seen in the legislation and programmes that have been implemented for cleaning up these rivers and river basins. In Taiwan, for example, the Environmental Protection Administration was established only in 1987, and one of its long range management programmes is to clean up the Tamshui River Basin in the north, around Taipei city (Baltierra, 1994, p. 1). As they pass through the Taipei basin, the waters of the river become heavily polluted with untreated domestic waste water, industrial and agricultural contaminants and a variety of other toxic pollutants. Pollution of Taiwan's rivers is mainly from pulp mills, dyeing factories, electroplating firms, pesticide manufacturing and food processing, but regulation and enforcement have been weak because of a lack of coordination between the Environmental Protection Administration and monitors from local government agencies (Baltierra 1994, p. 5).

Water pollution, due to the discharge of untreated or only partially treated human and factory effluent as well as solid waste disposal, has become a serious problem in many of the cities of Southeast Asia. The seas of Southeast Asia provide 11 per cent of the world's supply of marine products, but two of the major near-shore fishing areas in the region are over fished and receive discharges from both land based sources such as industries as well as accidental oil spills (United Nations, ESCAP, 1990; Uriarte, 1994, p. 1). Several countries, including the Philippines and Indonesia, have launched programmes to clean up their major rivers and river basins but success has varied greatly.

Deforestation is a major problem affecting Southeast Asia. Countries of insular Southeast Asia are losing their forests at the rate of 72 square metres per person per year, while the loss of forests in continental Southeast Asia is slightly higher at 74 square metres per person (World Resources Institute, 1994). In addition to deforestation, many mangrove areas in Southeast Asian countries are also being converted into either land for housing and industrial estates developments or brackish-water prawn farms producing for urban markets.

Judging from the rapid rate of population growth and urbanisation, there is every reason to anticipate that environmental issues will remain a major if not ever more important concern in Asia. Between 1960 and 1992, the population in the six member states of ASEAN grew by 200 per cent. Indonesia is one of the most populous countries in the world. The total population in these six countries grew from 160 millions in 1960 to 334 millions in 1992. By the year 2000, this total is expected to reach 381 millions or an increase of 12 per cent over the 1992 figure (UNDP Human Development Report, 1994). The rate of urbanisation in the ASEAN countries is not expected to be as rapid with a forecast rate of growth of 4.4 per cent in the years between 1992 and 2000. This, however, does not reflect past rates of urbanisation and, for example, the doubling (from 15 per cent to 30 per cent) of the urban population in Indonesia between 1960 and 1990.

The growth in urbanisation and industrialisation has been accompanied by equally dramatic increases in the demand for energy. During the period between 1980 and 1987, electricity consumption in Indonesia rose by 16 per cent annually. The demand for electricity in Thailand tripled in the 1980s, at a time when the annual growth of electricity consumption in Malaysia was 12 to 13 per cent. In the Philippines, the annual growth in demand was more modest, at less than 4 per cent between 1980 and 1990, because of slower economic growth. This illustrates the close link between economic development and the pressures placed on the physical environment in Southeast Asia.

Overall, growth in levels of energy consumption has had a major impact on the environment, and particularly air quality, in Southeast Asian cities. Per capita energy consumption as measured in kilograms of oil equivalent, has tripled in practically all the countries of ASEAN, except the Philippines. In Thailand, consumption has multiplied five-fold. This growth in energy consumption has been attributed to increases in the numbers of motor vehicles as well as the expansion of factories. The impact on air quality has been tremendous. Levels of suspended particulates dispersed in the atmosphere in Taipei County in Taiwan, for example, showed that the 1989 level was almost double that of 1975. The further escalation of the problem is shown by the fact that the amount of particulates in the air has further increased by 26 per cent since 1990 following the construction of Taipei's mass rapid transit system (Baltierra, 1994, p. 3). Levels of particulate pollution for similar years between 1975 and 1989 in major cities in South Korea like Seoul and Pusan, also remain close to or in excess of recommended environmental standards (Kwon 1992). Whereas, the World Health Organisation's current guidelines on acceptable daily levels recommend that the concentration of suspended particulates should be between 60 to 90 micrograms, many cities in the rapidly industrialising countries of Southeast Asia have levels that exceed 100 micrograms (UNEP Environmental Data Report, 1993-1994). The concentration of suspended particulates in the suburban industrial sites in Bangkok is 292 micrograms (also see Newman, 1993 and 1994)

Hawley (1986) has emphasised that complex urban ecosystem problems require people to come together as a polity to deal categorically with their needs and problems. While this has yet to happen in any of the rapidly industrialising economies in East and Southeast Asia, Singapore's experience with balancing industrialisation and environmental management has led to the recognition that 'enlightened elites and decision makers and firm government are the only ways to ensure the successful management and sustenance of viable urban ecosystems' (Savage and Kong, 1993, p. 38). Such a formula for tackling environmental issues in the city has exacted costs, both socio-political and physical, which are discussed in this chapter. The discussion highlights the dominance of the state in environmental management and the 'crowding out' of opportunities for participation by the public and the business sector in setting the agenda for environmental policy and action.

This kind of policy decision making process also implies the neglect of some areas of environmental management, as the following discussion will highlight.

The discussion that follows is focused on the industrialisation process in Singapore, its impact on that environment and the strategies that have been introduced to cope with that impact. In discussing these three themes, the central role of the state is made clear. The industrialisation drive was not only spearheaded by the state but was also supported by state provision of the infrastructure that development required. In contrast, the role of the private sector in environmental change in Singapore is very different. 'Private enterprise' according to Wong (1989, p. 775), 'involved in changing the physical environment is limited mainly to activities associated with private housing construction, site preparation for specific industries (such as oil refineries on Pulau Bukom and Pulau Ayer Chawan), and recreational areas such as golf courses'.

The physical environment of Singapore

Singapore is unique among rapidly industrialising countries in Asia because of its small area and equally small resource base. The country is made up of a main island and a number of surrounding smaller islands. Its entire area covers only 626 square kilometres. The changes to its physical environment had been slow and small scale until the launching of the industrialisation programme following independence, with large tracts of the original terrain swamps and coastline as well as offshore islands remaining relatively unchanged (Wong 1989, p. 772). Since the inception of the industrialisation programme, there have been major and rapid changes in the physical environment of Singapore. The nature of these changes has been summarised by Wong (1989, p. 774) using a framework modified from Douglas (1983). The environmental agents involved in these changes and their effects on Singapore's physical environment are outlined in Table 7.2.

The growth of the built-up area in Singapore has also brought about major physical environmental changes. 'Swamps, tidal wasteland and agricultural land have decreased significantly while the built-up area, including industrial sites, has increased at the expense of nearly all other land uses' (Wong, 1989, p. 772). This growth of the built-up area between 1960 and 1990 is illustrated in Table 7.3. Such changes in land-use distribution and land cover change are discussed below.

The industrialisation process in Singapore

The view that the role of the public sector in the Singapore economy does not appear to be overwhelming (Krause, 1987) has been supported by the opinion that the real influence of government in Singapore's economy has been to create and shape the conditions for economic development and

Table 7.2
Changes in the physical environment of Singapore

Environmental Agent	Effects on the Physical Environment
Urban raw materials	Extraction of granite, sand, and clay*
Urban climate	Urban microclimate Air pollution Acid rain
Hydrological cycle	Reservoirs* Regulated channels* Sediment production Floods*
Water pollution	Oil pollution Heavy-metals pollution
Waste disposal	Dumping grounds*
Landform	Slope failures Coastal landfill* Beaches*
Biogeography	Vegetation succession*

*   Major effect.

Source: Wong, 1989, p.774

ultimately to guide it, promote it, and harness it (Castells, et al., 1990, p. 179; Rodan, 1985). Singapore has been recognised as the quintessential 'development state', which Johnson (1982) has defined as the engine of hypergrowth in a group of economies headed by Japan and closely followed by South Korea and Taiwan. In these states, economic competitiveness has been a deliberately planned and engineered strategy that has been implemented by the national state (Gold, 1986). Through such strategies in Singapore,

> the government has provided industrial and business infrastructure: industrial estates, reclaimed land, port and air transportation facilities, telecommunications, auxiliary services for business transactions, and the like ... as well as effectiveness of their maintenance and of their management, [without which] Singapore's economy simply would not exist (Castells et al., 1990, p. 180).

Judging from growth of per capita GNP from US $800 in 1965, to US $12,543 some twenty-five years later, the industrialisation solution to Singapore's employment problems of the 1960s, appears to have been quite effective. Industrialisation, followed later by tourism, was the solution picked to solve the economic problems of the early years of self rule (Inter-Ministry Committee for the UNCED Preparatory Committee, 1992, p. 14). Unemployment rates fell from 5 per cent in the early 1970s to 3.6 per cent in 1978, and industry became as important an employer as the tertiary sector (Wong and Ooi, 1989, p. 804). By the 1980s, there was a labour shortage. Since the 1960s, the manufacturing sector has dominated the GDP (see Table 7.4).

The industrialisation drive in Singapore was heralded by the development of the Jurong industrial estate in 1961 on swamplands. Government agencies - the Economic Development Board and then the Jurong Town Corporation - transformed an area of ridges, swamps and coral-fringed coasts with relatively little development into the largest industrial estate in Singapore, an estate covering some 1,214 hectares or about 60 per cent of all land allocated to industry (Wong and Ooi, 1989, p. 794). Apart from site development and the provision of infrastructure, industry also received tax incentives to locate in the estate.

In Singapore, the growth in the manufacturing sector has been driven by multinational corporations (Chia, 1989; Grice and Drakakis-Smith, 1985). A comparison of the share of foreign ownership in the manufacturing sector between 1962 and 1985 highlights the growing dominance of foreign ownership and the reduction of local ownership to a mere fraction of its former share (see Table 7.5)

Because Singapore lacks a large natural resource base, the corporations encouraged by the government's incentives have primarily been those requiring a base for product assembly (such as electronics manufacturers) and access to regional markets. While in the 1960s, policy effort was directed at encouraging industries of all kinds, with incentives for labour intensive and import substitution enterprises, by the 1980s export-oriented industries were being given more encouragement (Wong and Ooi, 1989, p. 802). This

Table 7.3
Land-use distribution in Singapore, 1960-1990

Year	Total (a)		Forest		Swamp		Farm Holdings (b)		Built-Up Areas (c)		Others (d)	
	(sq km)	%	(sq km)	%	(sq km)	%	(sq km)	%	(sq km)	%	(sq km)	%
1960	581.5	100	37.8	6.5	45.9	7.9	141.7	24.4	162.3	27.9	193.8	33.3
1965	581.5	100	35.0	6.0	35.0	6.0	131.6	22.6	177.4	30.5	205.5	33.5
1970	584.6	100	32.4	5.5	32.4	5.5	134.0	22.9	189.9	32.4	197.7	33.7
1975	596.8	100	32.4	5.4	32.4	5.4	105.9	17.7	228.4	38.3	197.7	33.1
1980	617.8	100	30.0	4.9	26.0	4.2	80.9	13.1	275.1	44.5	205.8	33.3
1985	620.2	100	28.6	4.6	18.7	3.0	58.9	9.5	295.0	47.6	219.0	35.3
1990	633.1	100	28.6	4.5	15.7	2.5	10.8	1.7	311.6	49.2	266.4	42.1

(a) Percentages do not necessarily sum to 100 because of the rounding out of some figures.

(b) Licensed farms, excluding land under pure rubber and coconut plantations.

(c) Includes new industrial estates.

(d) Includes inland water, open spaces, public gardens, cemeteries, non-built up areas in military establishments, quarries, rubber and coconut plantations, and unused land.

Sources: Tyabji 1993, p.131; Wong 1989, p.774

Table 7.4
Share of industry in GDP (at 1985 market prices)

	1960	1970	1980	1990	Average Annual Rate of Growth*
Quarrying	0.22	0.23	0.23	0.18	7.1
Manufacturing	16.59	24.82	29.48	28.56	10.8
Utilities	1.71	1.93	2.00	2.10	9.5
Construction	5.27	9.47	7.13	5.78	8.7
Total	23.79	36.45	38.84	36.62	

* GDP grew at 8.7 per cent during 1960-1990.
Source: Tyabji 1993, p.126

Table 7.5
Share of foreign investment in the manufacturing sector, 1962-85

Year	Percentage Share of Ownership	Gross Output	Value Added	Employment	Direct Exports
1962	Wholly foreign-owned	31.4	24.6	14.1	26.3
	More than half foreign-owned				
	Less than half foreign-owned	23.0	27.9	19.6	29.0
	Wholly local-owned	45.6	47.5	66.4	44.7
	Total	100.0	100.0	100.0	100.0
1965	Wholly foreign-owned	29.2	28.2	12.1	32.1
	More than half foreign-owned				
	Less than half foreign-owned	32.0	29.5	26.5	32.8
	Wholly local-owned	38.8	42.4	61.4	35.1
	Total	100.0	100.0	100.0	100.0
1970	Wholly foreign-owned	43.4	37.0	17.7	56.7
	More than half foreign-owned	12.4	12.4	17.0	
	Less than half foreign-owned	13.2	15.0	20.0	26.8
	Wholly local-owned	31.0	35.6	45.3	16.5
	Total	100.0	100.0	100.0	100.0
1975	Wholly foreign-owned	56.2	47.4	31.5	66.1
	More than half foreign-owned	15.1	15.3	20.5	18.0
	Less than half foreign-owned	10.7	13.0	15.1	7.0
	Wholly local-owned	18.0	24.3	32.8	8.9
	Total	100.0	100.0	100.0	100.0
1980	Wholly foreign-owned	58.7	54.1	39.9	71.5
	More than half foreign-owned	15.0	13.3	18.5	13.2
	Less than half foreign-owned	10.7	13.5	13.5	8.2
	Wholly local-owned	15.6	19.1	28.1	7.1
	Total	100.0	100.0	100.0	100.0
1985	Wholly foreign-owned	54.5	54.9	41.6	65.7
	More than half foreign-owned	15.9	9.9	11.8	16.5
	Less than half foreign-owned	9.3	11.8	13.1	6.4
	Wholly local-owned	20.3	23.4	33.5	11.4
	Total	100.0	100.0	100.0	100.0

Source: Chia 1989, p.261

Table 7.6
Top ten industries in manufacturing, 1991-1993

	1993 Value Added (% Share)	1991	1992	1993[2]
		Percentage Change Over Previous Year		
INDEX OF INDUSTRIAL PRODUCTION (1992 = 100)				
Total Manufacturing[1]	100.0	5.4	2.5	9.8
Electronic Products	40.9	-	8.8	23.0
Transport Equipment	7.2	4.8	-0.3	-0.8
Petroleum Products	7.0	3.3	0.8	13.8
Fabricated Metal Products	6.4	0.8	5.7	3.7
Paints, Pharmaceutical & Other Chemical Products	5.3	31.0	-8.4	3.2
Machinery except Electrical & Electronic	5.0	12.9	-0.8	-6.5
Printing & Publishing	4.8	8.6	7.2	8.0
Electrical Machinery, Apparatus & Appliances	3.8	9.0	0.1	3.4
Industrial Chemicals & Gases	3.0	1.8	-5.0	5.0
Food	2.4	5.4	2.7	3.8

[1]   Excluding rubber processing
[2]   Provisional figures

Source: Ministry of Trade and Industry 1994, p.55

attempt to restructure manufacturing in Singapore was partly in response to increased competition from low wage countries, but also in response to continuing labour shortages and slow growth in labour productivity (Chia, 1989, p. 263).   Consequently, there was a shift from labour intensive industries such as food, clothing and furniture manufacture to high technology and high value added manufacture such as, petrochemicals, precision instruments and production of industrial equipment. By 1993, a new and distinctive industrial structure had been developed as is demonstrated in the figures of Table 7.6 relating to the ten most important sectors in the Singapore economy measured in terms of share of value added. Electronics production dominates the production of value added, contributing 40.9 per cent of all value added from manufacturing. What is more, electronics production is continuing to expand rapidly. In contrast, food production contributes only 2.4 per cent of manufacturing value added and, comparatively, is growing only slowly.

The preoccupation with economic performance has been reflected in the development agenda which has guided state planners, both economic and physical, in Singapore. According to the Inter-Ministry Committee which compiled the national report for the Earth Summit (1992):

> The principles guiding Singapore's environmental policies can be summarised in ... order of priority [as]:
>
> a.   Satisfy the people's economic needs first;
> b.   Control population growth;
> c.   Prevent pollution at source;
> d.   Conduct Environmental Impact Assessment (EA) for all development projects;
> e.   Educate the public;
> f.   Legislate;
> g.   Enforce;
> h.   Monitor and review. (p.9)

The priorities of this environmental management programme help to explain the relative neglect of another significant aspect of environmental protection - nature conservation. Until recently, this neglect has gone unchallenged largely because the state, working with the more limited priorities outlined above, set the agenda for environmental management.

Environmental impact and policy in Singapore

Industrialisation, and the parallel process of urban growth in Singapore, has had significant impacts on the local physical environments. These impacts have been both direct and indirect. The direct impacts include air and water pollution, the development of land for industrial estates, and the provision of all types of infrastructure needed to support industrial activities. Indirect impacts include the demand for land to house workers employed in new industries, and the provision that must be made to meet their transport needs.

Singapore's industrialisation peaked in the early 1970s (Inter-Ministry Committee for the UNCED Preparatory Committee, 1992), as did levels of emissions of air pollutants (Figures 7.1 to 7.4). The negative impacts on air quality in particular and the physical environment in general, prompted the government to form the Anti-Pollution Unit in 1970 and the Ministry of Environment in 1972. The former was established to control air pollution while the latter was charged with overseeing water pollution and the management of solid wastes. In 1986, the Anti-Pollution Unit was incorporated into the Ministry of Environment.

State agencies in Singapore have been supported by the necessary state legislation to carry out their work. Effective implementation of such legislation has resulted in a lowering of levels of air pollutants. The Clean Air Act (1971) and the Clean Air (Standards) Regulations (1972) are examples of the legislation introduced to control air pollution. These regulations have seen revisions and tightening over time. The success of these regulations is demonstrated in Figures 7.1 to 7.4 for levels of total acidity, smoke, nitrogen oxide and dust fall out. Acidity levels fell in the 1970s and 1980s but that improvement has levelled off. Urban smoke levels continue to decline (Figure 7.2), but nitrogen oxide levels have been far more variable (Figure 7.3). Dust fall out deteriorated in the 1970s and recorded consistent reductions only after 1983.

Essentially, environmental policy in Singapore has been gradualist in its approach, and amendments to the legislation on air pollution control illustrate this aspect of environmental management. Environmental standards have become stricter and more stringent over time. So when emission standards were raised in the late 1970s, existing factories were required to fit pollution control equipment but new factories were not allowed to start operations until they had the appropriate equipment installed.

The Ministry of Environment must be consulted when any industrial investment is being considered in Singapore and before any factory is actually allocated land for development (Inter-Ministry Committee for the UNCED Preparatory Committee, 1992, p.19). However, while environmental policy has been shaped and implemented by the Ministry of Environment, efforts have been made to coordinate with other government agencies to control pollution at its sources. The regulation of car ownership is an example of the efforts made jointly by the Ministry of Environment, the Registry of Vehicles and the Traffic Police to control smoke emission in Singapore. Tough policy measures have been introduced to discourage not only car ownership but also the use of cars. As alternatives, public transport has been developed. In addition to a comprehensive network of roads and expressways linking homes to industrial estates and the commercial centres - the workplaces and service centres of the city - there are taxi cab companies, two major public bus

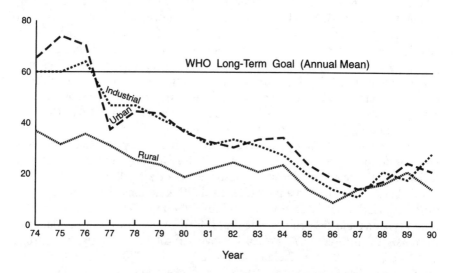

Figure 7.1 Air Pollution Levels, 1974-1990: Total Acidity Levels
Microgram per cubic metre at normal temperature and pressure

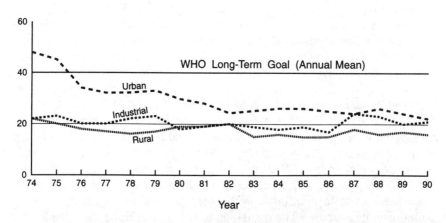

Figure 7.2 Air Pollution Levels, 1974-1990: Smoke Levels
Microgram per cubic metre at normal temperature and pressure

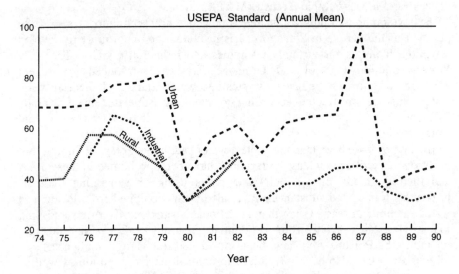

Figure 7.3   Air Pollution Levels, 1974-1990:   Nitrogen Oxide Levels
Microgram per cubic metre at normal temperature and pressure

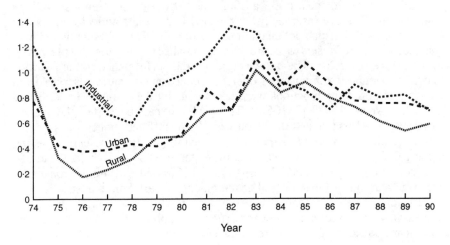

Figure 7.4   Air Pollution Levels, 1974-1990:   Dust Fallout Levels
Grams per square metre per month

companies, a number of smaller bus operators who serve schools and certain offices, and a Mass Rapid Transit (MRT) system.

The development of public housing, which currently accommodates some 86 per cent of the people in Singapore, has provided the opportunity to develop sewerage facilities for virtually all homes and industrial estates. The 1975 Water Pollution Control and Drainage Act was introduced to prevent discharge of human or industrial wastes into water courses. Industrial waste water must be pre-treated according to standards stipulated by the Trade Effluent Regulations of 1976 before discharge into a sewer or any watercourse.

Great pains have been taken to protect water catchment areas. Polluting, but traditional activities, such as pig farming, have been prohibited in these areas and then gradually phased out. Industries using or generating toxic or hazardous wastes and substances have also been prohibited from locating in water catchment areas. Often they are allocated sites on offshore islands and industrial estates away from residential locations. Legal instruments, including the Poisons Act, have been introduced to ensure compliance.

Legislation has also been introduced to control marine pollution as well as to preserve nature reserves. Progress in reducing levels of pollution such as the faecal coliform count has, unfortunately, not been matched in the area of nature conservation.

The expansion of the built -up area, associated with rapid industrialisation and urban growth, has been accompanied by the deletion as well as degradation of nature reserves first protected under the Nature Reserves Act introduced by the British colonial administration in 1951. When this law was enacted, a Nature Reserves Board was established to oversee the protection of the nature reserves. The bitter verdict on the performance of the Board is that it '... actually administered over the reduction of nature reserves from five to two before its functions were taken over by the National Parks Board in 1990' (Wee, 1993, p. 106). The problem had been that the Nature Reserves Board had lacked the resources - both staff and money - to perform anything other than an advisory role. A major mangrove reserve covering some 1,012 hectares when it was first protected in 1884, had dwindled to 556 hectares some 50 years later (Wee, 1993, p. 106) and in 1982 the remaining area was reassigned for industrial development. Apart from industrialisation, infrastructure development - telecommunications, reservoirs, quarrying, expressways and recreational spaces such as public parks - has meant that significant portions of existing reserves have been 'sterilised'. The status of the remaining reserves, though protected by the National Parks Act, remains precarious, not only ecologically but also legally. This problem was highlighted recently when it was proposed to develop part of the largest remaining nature reserve into a golf course. This was an important event because it heralded the emergence of a new force in Singapore's environmental questions - non-government organisations.

The role of non-government organisations in Singapore

The golf course proposal spurred the non-government organisation, the Nature Society, to mount a month long study and environmental impact assessment to appeal against the development of the golf course. Such active non-government effort had not been characteristic of the agenda for environmental management. 'Prior to 1980, non-government organisation activity in the environmental arena was minimal' (Inter-Ministry Committee for the UNCED Preparatory Committee, 1992, p. 50). The success of the Nature Society in staying the proposal to develop the golf course in the nature reserve area coincided with the political leadership's move towards more public participation in policy decision making. Negotiations between the Nature Society and state agencies led to the watershed decision for an 87 hectare site to be set aside for conservation. This success represented a landmark for nature conservationists from this non-government organisation because it was the first land site allocated for conservation since Singapore had gained self-rule from the colonial British.

A master plan for nature conservation was compiled by the Nature Society. This has eventually won the support of the Ministry of Environment which has encouraged other government agencies to incorporate the recommendations made in the plan.

The Ministry of Environment has actually encouraged the establishment of the National Council on the Environment (NCE) which has a secretariat located in the same building as the Ministry:

> The NCE is a private voluntary organisation formed with the blessing of the Government, and run by leading corporate entrepreneurs. Its objectives are to involve the private sector in the promotion of greater public awareness of and concern for the living environment and environmental protection measures, in making representations to the Government for legislation in support of its objectives, and in cooperation with other similar organisations, both local and foreign (The Inter-Ministry Committee for the UNCED Preparatory Committee 1992, p. 55).

There has been scepticism about the role that businesses and industries are prepared to contribute to environmental management (Kong, 1993, p.15). Such scepticism has some basis judging from the dominance of the state in setting the agenda for environmental policy and action in the last three decades. Like the public, firms in Singapore are driven by the profit motive and business considerations which have, to date, not made it necessary for corporations generally to emphasise environmentally friendly behaviour in order to maintain or improve market share. The few corporations that have emphasised environmental goals have been multinationals run by Chief Executive Officers with personal commitment to environmental protection. Nevertheless, non-government environmental organisations in Singapore have only small memberships. The membership of the Nature Society is in the order of only 1,000 people. Active participation in environmental programmes remains limited among the people of Singapore as does environmental consciousness.

Perhaps realising that long term environmental management requires stronger commitment from the public, and that consciousness of the need for environmental protection can only be established if these values are instilled in people, the Ministry of Environment has increased its efforts to encourage Singaporeans to be more environment friendly and environmentally aware. Working with non-government organisations and encouraging businesses to be more active reflects their effort. It represents a departure from the traditional use of regulatory punitive measures to ensure compliance with environmental policy - 'a litany of laws and fines' (Kong, 1993, p. 7)

Conclusions

Economic success through rapid industrialisation in many East and Southeast Asian countries has exacted tremendous environmental costs. In Singapore, which has given as much priority to economic growth as the other newly industrialising countries, the 'development state' has varied somewhat in its concern with environmental protection and management. Emphasis has, however, been given to anti-pollution measures and infrastructural development.

There has been neglect of areas such as nature conservation which has in turn, encouraged the more active participation of non-government organisations in environmental management. At the same time, the dominant role which the state has played in the agenda for environmental policy and action also implied that success has been achieved because of the fear of legal and monetary indictments (Ministry of Communications and Information, 1990). Effort to correct the apathy evident among the public and even the business community has been initiated by the state itself through the Ministry of Environment.

The process of encouraging greater collaboration and public participation is compromised by the state's continuing role in setting the environmental agenda. This implies that while it is seeking the greater involvement of non-government organisations and business in implementing its programmes, the policy decision making process remains centralised within the state and lacks the transparency required for collaboration to be taken more seriously. While the observation has been made that 'in highly concentrated large urban nodes such as Singapore, the onus of maintaining harmonious human environment relationships cannot be left to *ad hoc* spontaneous actions' (Kong, 1993, p.15), the participation of the public and business has evolved in such an ad hoc way.

Changes, however, are being made. These are evident in the effort that has been initiated by the Ministry of Environment to incorporate the Nature Society's recommendations on conservation into development plans, together with the bid to involve business more actively in environmental protection. The collaboration with the private sector, non-government organisations and consumers, is reflective of the state's recognition that, as the costs of environmental management services and protection work rise, there is advantage to be gained from sharing the responsibility for them. If the responsibility is to be shared by the non-government sector, however, it can be expected to demand a bigger say in environmental policy decision making.

Notes

1. ASEAN member states include Brunei, Indonesia, Malaysia, Philippines, Singapore and Thailand.

References

Baltierra, M. (1994), 'River basin pollution control', paper presented to the Second Leadership Seminar on Sustainable Urban Environment in Southeast Asia, Kuala Lumpur, October 2-3.

Castells, M., Goh, L.E. and Kwok, RY-W. (1990), *The Shek Kip Mei Syndrome - Economic Development and Public Housing in Hong Kong*, Pion, London.

Chia, S.Y. (1989), 'Industrialisation', in K.S. Sandu and P. Wheatley (eds), 'The Management of Success - Moulding of Modern Singapore, Institute of Southeast Asian Studies, Singapore, pp. 250-279.

Douglas, I. (1983), *The Urban Environment*, Edward Arnold, London.

Gold, T. (1986), *State and Society in Taiwan's Economic Miracle*, Sharpe, Armond, New York.

Grice, K. and Drakakis-Smith, D. (1985), 'The role of the state in shaping development: two decades of growth in Singapore', *Transactions, Institute of British Geographers*, vol. 10, pp. 347-359.

Hawley, A.H. (1986), *Human Ecology*, Chicago University Press, Chicago.

Inter-Ministry Committee for UNCED Preparatory Committee, Singapore's National Report for the 1992 UN Conference on Environment and Development Preparatory Committee, Singapore.

Johnson, C. (1982), *MITI and the Japanese Miracle*, Stanford University Press, Stanford.

Kilmartin, L., Thorns, D. and Burke, T. (1985) *Social Theory and the Australian City*, George Allen & Unwin, Sydney.

Kong, L. (1993), 'Environment as a social concern: democratising 'public arenas' in Singapore?' Paper presented at the Workshop on 'Democracy and Development in an Ecological Era,' Information and Resource Centre, December 2-3, Singapore.

Krause, L.B. (1987), 'The government as an entrepreneur', in Krause, L.B.,

Koh, Ai Tee, and Lee, Tsao Yuan (eds), *The Singapore Economy Reconsidered*, Institute of Southeast Asian Studies, Singapore, pp. 107-127.Kwon, S. (1992), 'A survey of quality of life in the ESCAP region: the Republic of Korea,' KDI Working Paper No. 9211, Korea Development Institute.

Lee, S.A. (1973), *Industrialisation in Singapore*, Longman, Melbourne.

Newman, P. (1994), 'The transport dilemma in developing nation cities', in Jayasariya, L. and Lee, M. (eds), *Social Dimensions of Development*, Paradigm Books, Perth, Australia, pp. 89-108.

Newman, P. (1993), 'Cities and Development - an emerging Asian model,' *Development Bulletin*, vol.27, pp. 20-22.

Nijathaworn, B. and Vongpradhip, D. (1993), 'ASEAN economic overview and outlook,' in Koomsup, F. (ed.) *Economic Development and the Environment in ASEAN Countries Proceedings of the Sixteenth*

Conference of the Federation of ASEAN Economic Associations, 28-30 November 1991, Bangkok, Thailand, pp. 1-18.

Rodan, G. (1985), 'Singapore's second industrial revolution: state intervention and foreign investments', Australia Research Project, Association of Southeast Asian Nations, Kuala Lumpur and Canberra.

Samah, A.A. (1994), 'Atmospheric quality - a striving for clean air in urban areas', paper presented to the Second Leadership Seminar on 'Towards a sustainable urban environment in Southeast Asia', October 3-5, Kuala Lumpur, Malaysia.

Savage, V. and Kong, L. (1993), 'Urban constraints, political imperatives: environmental design in Singapore', *Landscape and Urban Planning,* vol. 25, pp. 37-52.

The Economist. (1991)   Asia's Emerging Economies, *The Economist Newspaper,* November 16, pp. 19.

Tyabji, A. (1993), 'Industry and environment in Singapore', in Koomsup, P. (ed.)   *Economic Development and the Environment in ASEAN Countries, Proceedings of the Sixteenth Conference of the Federation of ASEAN Economic Associations,* 28-30 November 1991, Bangkok Thailand, p. 125-150.

UNDP (United Nations Development Program) (1994), *Human Development Report, 1994,* Oxford Univeristy Press, New York.

UNEP (United Nations Environmental Program) (1994) *Environmental Data Report, 1993-94,* Blackwell, London.

UN ESCAP (1990), *The State of the Environment in Asia and the Pacific,* United Nations, Bangkok, Thailand.

Uriarte, Jr., F.A. (1994), 'Sustainable development: ASEAN policies and programmes', Paper presented to the Second Leadership Seminar on 'Towards a sustainable urban environment in Southeast Asia, October 2-3, Kuala Lumpur, Malaysia.

Wee, Y.C. (1993), 'Coping with nature and nature conservation in Singapore', in Briffett, C. and Sim, L.L. (eds) *Proceedings: Environmental Issues in Development and Conservation,* School of Building and Estate Management, National University of Singapore, Singapore , pp. 103-108.

Wong, P.P. (1989), 'Transformation of the physical environment', in Sandhu, K.S. and Wheatley, P. (eds) *The Management of Success - Moulding of Modern Singapore,* Institute of Southeast Asian Studies, Singapore, pp. 771-787.

Wong, A.K. and Ooi, G.L., (1989) 'Spatial reorganisation', in Sandhu, K.S. and Wheatley, P. (eds) *The Management of Success - Moulding of Modern Singapore.* Institute of Southeast Asian Studies, Singapore, pp. 788-812.

World Resources Institute (1994), *World Resources, 1994,* World Resources Institute, Washington, DC.

8 Local government, environmental policy and economic development

David Gibbs and Michael Healey

Introduction

One of the major current policy issues in local economic development is how to match the growth of interest in environmental issues and sustainable development with the perceived need for employment and income generation. However, while there is general agreement that sustainability is a 'good thing', there has only recently been any attempt to explore the implications of sustainable development for local economic development (Local Government Management Board, 1993; Haughton and Hunter, 1994). It has been argued that sustainable development will largely be implemented through the actions of local authorities which are ideally placed to formulate a multi-level corporate strategy for the sustainable management of the local environment' (Local Government Management Board, 1992, p. 2). In this chapter, the international and national policy contexts for the work of UK local authorities is outlined and some of the implications for local economic development are explored. The overall argument that emerges from this evaluation is that achieving sustainable development in local economies will necessitate substantial change in the nature and direction of these economies. However, contrary to neo-liberal belief that the market is the most effective mechanism for achieving this change, it is argued that there needs to be a legislative and policy framework in place to stimulate and direct change. A key message that emerges in this chapter is the need for more active engagement by central government.

Sustainable development

Early debates over the tensions between the environment and economic development assumed that the future meant either economic growth or 'no growth' (the classic example of which was the 1972 Club of Rome report, *The Limits to Growth*). In recent years these tensions have supposedly been resolved through the adoption of sustainable development as a guiding principle. Although sustainable development is a concept that has been around in various guises for some years, it acquired popular momentum with the publication in 1987 of *Our Common Future*, the report of the United Nations World Commission on Environment and Development, or the Brundtland Report as it has commonly come to be called. Sustainable development, in the definition utilised by the World Commission, 'meets the needs of the present, without compromising the ability of future generations to meet their own needs' (World Commission on Environment and Development, 1987, p. 43). The 1992 United Nations Conference on Environment and Development (UNCED) held in Rio de Janeiro (the 'Earth Summit') reaffirmed this political and moral commitment to sustainable development by national governments, mainly through the 'blueprint for action' of Agenda 21. This definition has been adopted by many national governments as the basis for future economic development, as it appears to enable the integration of economic and environmental aims (Department of the Environment, 1993). For example, in the United Kingdom the Department of the Environment's Planning Policy Guidance (PPG) for local authorities explicitly directs UK local authorities to produce development plans based on sustainable development principles (PPG 12: Development Plans and Regional Policy Guidance) and emphasises the desirability of reducing the need to travel and better integration of land use planning and transport provision (PPG 13: Transport).

A useful distinction can be made between *'weak'* and *'strong'* forms of sustainability (Daly and Cobb, 1989; Gibbs and Healey, 1994). In the former, environmental concerns assume a higher priority in economic policy, but there is no specification of the environmental quality to be achieved. With *weak* sustainability, the emphasis will effectively be on raising environmental efficiency i.e., reducing the environmental impact of each unit of economic activity. It addresses individual parts of the economy, such as firms or sectors, but does not have a holistic approach to the environment. The *strong* version of sustainability, however, specifies minimum levels of environmental quality to be achieved prior to the consideration of other goals. The *strong* version begins from a presumption that society cannot simply let economic activity result in a continual decline in the quality and functions of the environment, even though it may be beneficial in other ways (Jacobs and Stott, 1992). In this version of sustainable development there are lower limits to environmental quality such that a sustainable economy is a constrained economy (Jacobs, 1991). *Strong* sustainable development will require targets to be set for environmental impacts such as emission levels and measures taken to constrain firms and individuals to ensure that these targets are met such that the whole of the economy is affected, rather than some of its constituent parts (Jacobs and Stott, 1992). This distinction between *weak* and *strong* versions of sustainability is important because of the implications for understanding how implementing sustainable development will affect the economy.

Adopting a *strong* version of sustainable development as the basis of economic development necessitates a number of changes in the way in which we think about development. First, it involves the integration of environmental and economic policy, so that the conflicts between them are not hidden but are resolved within a common framework. Second, the concept of development broadens from one emphasising growth to one incorporating notions of economic welfare, encompassing non-financial elements. Thus, sustainable development means that environmental quality can improve economic development through, for example, improving the health of the work force and creating jobs in environmentally related sectors of the economy. Sustainable development is not, therefore, solely concerned with a growth in real incomes. Finally, the concept of sustainable development incorporates a commitment to equity. That is not just the creation of wealth and the conservation of resources, but also their fair distribution. The notion of equity should operate not just inter-generationally, but also intra-generationally. Clearly, a commitment to equity necessitates greater public participation and democratic action (WCED, 1987).

The policy context

A better understanding of sustainability at the local level is important because a major role for local authorities is envisaged in existing international and national policy statements (OECD, 1990). For example, implementing the Agenda 21 principles agreed at the 1992 Rio de Janeiro Earth Summit can only take place with the active involvement of local authorities and communities (Bosworth, 1993; UNCED, 1992). In Europe much of the context for environmental policy making is increasingly set by legislation from the European Union (EU) (Bennett, 1992). The Fifth Environmental Action Programme (1993-2000), entitled *Towards Sustainability*, stresses the need for a more proactive approach in order to alter behavioural patterns and encourage a move towards sustainable development (CEC, 1992). The implications for local economies of EU actions are substantial (CEC, 1990). EU legislation effectively creates the starting point and a base level from which local proactive strategies can proceed. The Commission envisages that much of the responsibility for integrating economic development with environmental protection at the local level will rest with local government, particularly through the planning process. A number of key areas are identified within the Fifth Environmental Action Programme where local authorities can play a role: spatial planning; economic development; infrastructure development; control of industrial pollution; waste management; transport; public information, education and training; and internal auditing. In total, environmental policy has an enhanced status within the EU such that the Fifth Environmental Action Programme proposes that environmental protection be included as an objective of all other policies. However, it should be pointed out that there are major contradictions between such environmental objectives and other EU policies and programmes (Gibbs, 1993b).

While EU legislation has had an important recent impact, local authorities in the UK have a long history of responsibility for their local environment, dating back to the nineteenth century. However, more recent national legislation has also brought their environmental responsibilities to the forefront of discussion. Both the White Paper, *The Common Inheritance* and the Environmental Protection Act (1990) confirmed existing environmental responsibilities and defined new ones for local authorities. A number of areas for local authority action were outlined in the White Paper, mostly in terms of 'encouragement' and 'awareness' rather than being prescriptive. For example, local authorities were expected to encourage energy efficiency measures, to take greater account of environmental considerations in planning and development decisions, to protect open space and discourage out-of-town development, and to consider the traffic implications of development.

Both the White Paper and the Environmental Protection Act can be criticised for lacking clear targets for environmental improvement and for failing to develop a long-term vision of the UK's environment. The White Paper, which promised to set out a strategy for the UK's environment, made little attempt to introduce the kinds of long-term integrated policy measures which would back the claim made within it that government policy is based on concepts of sustainable development. The Environmental Protection Act consisted of a number of piecemeal measures which do not adequately address the problems of enforcement and resources for implementation. Government follow-ups to the White Paper have emphasised the need to incorporate sustainable development into the planning process at all stages of development and to implement the Earth Summit's Agenda 21 (HM Government, 1992). However, the UK sustainable development strategy provides little indication of a clear sense of direction by central government or a commitment to set targets and timetables for such action, but rather emphasises that the government will rely on economic instruments rather than regulation to deliver environmental objectives (HM Government, 1994).

The major role of local authorities in delivering sustainable development has, therefore, been recognised by a variety of bodies both at the international and national scales. It is obvious that one of the major influences to create a sustainable local economy will come from legislation emanating from the EU as well as that enacted by the UK government. The Fifth Environmental Section Programme is a clear indication of the EU's intent to shift the basis of future European development onto sustainable development. Furthermore it is also clear that the EU regards local authorities as one of the major players in policy delivery and enforcement. However, how the Programme is to be turned into effective, practical policy actions is much less clear. Similarly, UK government policy makes claims to be based upon sustainable development and envisages a lead role for local authorities in implementing it:

However, the lack of an adequate regulatory framework from national government, the lack of sufficient resources specifically for monitoring and environment protection work by local authorities, and the lack of resources for local authorities generally are all hampering the ability of local authorities to carry out their key role. It reveals the irony of the British Government's vocal demands on subsidiarity that they are prepared to give local authorities this key role, but not to provide them with the powers and resources to carry out this role adequately. (Bosworth, 1993, p. 17)

A role for local authorities

Despite the absence of a strong lead from national government, there has been considerable activity in developing policy around sustainability issues and examining the practical implications of sustainable development for local economies, both by local authority representative bodies and local authorities themselves. Much of this activity has been galvanised by the Local Agenda 21 process and increasingly involves networking between local authorities, particularly in Europe. Such initiatives include the International Council for Local Environmental Initiative's Local Agenda 21 Communities Network of local governments and their partners who are undertaking sustainable development planning processes and the European Conference on Cities and Towns. The conference, held in Aalborg in 1994, established the European Sustainable Cities and Towns Campaign, the Charter of which commits 80 European Cities to establish local action plans using the Local Agenda 21 approach (ICEI, 1994).

A major role within the UK is being played by the Local Government Management Board (LGMB), both in its own right as a coordinating body promoting United Nations and EU environmental initiatives and good environmental practice (see LGMB, 1993, for example), and through the LGMB acting as the location for the Local Agenda 21 officer appointed to undertake the work of the inter-organisational Local Agenda 21 Steering Group. The UK's Local Agenda 21 response is managed by a Steering Group drawn from the UK local authority associations and is serviced by LGMB. The Steering Group's current Chair is from the Association of District Councils (ADC), with the remainder of the Group drawn from elected members representing the ADC, the Association of County Councils, the Association of Metropolitan Authorities, the Convention of Scottish Local Authorities and the Association of Local Authorities in Northern Ireland, together with representatives from a range of public and private sector bodies. The work of the Steering Group so far has been to:

• publish a summary of Agenda 21 for local authorities;
• respond to the UK Strategy for Sustainable Development;
• produce the UK local government declaration on sustainable

development; and

- produce round table guidance notes on community participation, North/South linking, education and awareness raising, the transport/planning interface, green purchasing and compulsory competitive tendering and greening economic development.

A pilot project to develop local indicators for sustainability involved six projects in Cardiff City Council, Fife Regional Council, Hertfordshire County Council, Mendip District Council, Oldham Metropolitan Borough Council and the London Borough of Merton.

In addition to this collective action, many local authorities have turned to devising and implementing their own strategies. From an initial focus on audits and state of the environment reports, some authorities have progressed to the implementation stage where issues of sustainable development become important. Jacobs (1993) points out that there have been three phases of local environmental policy. In phase one, policy is unintegrated and there is no corporate approach to the environment as a whole. In phase two, environmental policy comes to the forefront and is considered in a more holistic manner. It is this phase, which developed throughout the 1980s, when several local authorities began to develop their own 'green' strategies. These phase two initiatives essentially represented a passive response, involving internal audits of local authority practice and state of the environment reports, appraising the condition of the local environment (Street, 1992).

However, such assessments of environmental problems within a local area represent an essential starting point in developing proactive environmental policies. From audits and assessments it is possible to formulate strategy and identify specific areas for remedial action and establish the major priorities for environmental monitoring. This forms phase three of Jacobs' three stage process whereby local authorities begin to develop sustainability goals. The earlier phases remain important, however, as they provide the indicators necessary to monitor progress towards sustainable development. This process of greater awareness can essentially be seen as involving a move from weak to stronger forms of sustainability.

In reassessing their economic development functions in the light of sustainable development, what are the forms of development and initiative that local authorities should be concerned with? Hams et al., (1994) define the key implications for economic development as:

> encouraging the development, manufacture, promotion and use of clean technologies and processes such as those which minimise resource use: minimise waste production; avoid and minimise pollution; re-use or recycle wastes; clean up past pollution or environmental damage; measure and monitor the state of the environment. It is also important to monitor and regulate the environmental performance of industry in ways that prevent environmental damage and environmental

improvement; create employment; and raise awareness and understanding of environmental issues in the business community and encourage responsible attitudes. (p. 40)

Indeed, a whole spectrum of measures from *weak* to *strong* can be identified to help implement sustainable development within a local economy. At their simplest such measures can help to make the local environment more attractive. The sorts of measures here relate to cutting down the unpleasant aspects of life, such as litter and pollution, through to reduced traffic congestion (Gibbs, 1991). These are perhaps the traditional environmental improvements that local administrations can implement. However, there is a broader range of issues which creates opportunities for local administrations. Realising some of these opportunities would involve redirecting a local economy by adapting more traditional economic development strategies, although in new formats - for example, a science park for environmental technologies, building upon local higher education institution strengths to improve links with firms in environmental areas, or using venture capital funds to target 'green' companies (see Gibbs, 1993a and LGMB, 1993 for more detailed outlines of potential initiatives). These initiatives essentially represent *weak* sustainability measures, while other *stronger* options could take a more holistic view and aim to indicate future directions towards sustainable development for the economy as a whole.

A *weak* sustainability approach would concentrate upon improving environmental efficiency at the level of individual firms or sectors; that is reducing the environmental impact of each unit of economic activity (Jacobs and Stott, 1992). By contrast, strong sustainability would aim to introduce sustainability planning, set targets for the major environmental problems in an area and then intervene to ensure these targets are met (Jacobs and Stott, 1992). To date, the major local strategies, in the UK at least, fall into the former category.

The Local Government Management Board (1993) identifies five possible aims which might act as the basis for an integrated approach to environmental and economic strategies:

- helping businesses to reduce their impacts on the environment;
- encouraging a move towards a more sustainable mix of businesses in the area, for example through inward investment (Gibbs, 1994a);
- fostering the development of an environmental industry in the local area (Stott, 1993);
- protecting the environment in ways that do not threaten jobs; and
- seeking business opportunities through environmental protection and enhancement
  (Gibbs, 1994b).

However, these are areas of sustainable development which, until recently, have received little attention. In the longer term, moreover, there are a number of issues in developing such policies which need to be addressed. In particular, there is a tension between policies which focus on sustainable local economic development and the evidence that local economies are increasingly integrated into, and depend on, global economic development. It may well be that it is impossible to redirect the dominant capitalist system into a more environmentally sustainable form. This certainly cannot be achieved by local level action alone (Haughton and Hunter, 1994).

Despite this concern, the types of policies which are currently being developed may represent 'way stages' in the shift to a more sustainable local economy (Gibbs, 1991). There is some evidence that authorities in the UK have begun to move into Jacob's phase three of local environmental policy. For example, out of the Kirklees State of the Environment Report has come the Kirklees Environment Initiative with a number of Environmental Action Programmes, developed as part of the Council's Local Agenda 21 initiative, intended to turn the broad goals of an Environment Strategy into action. These detailed action programmes, with over 400 specification points are being drawn together to form a Council-wide document setting out specific aims, measurable performance targets, responsible officers and units and resource implications. Other projects include:

- a study to ascertain how sustainable development can be incorporated into local decision making on transport policy and energy use;
- the 'Green Corridors' project to develop, protect and manage green corridors and to inform policy development for Kirklees' Unitary Development Plan;
- an Environmental Innovation Budget to fund local authority and voluntary environmental work on energy, transport, health and environmental awareness; and
- an Environment Forum to bring together members of the public, local environmental groups and the business community and to create issue-specific working groups which can report back into the Council's decision making process (personal communication, Environment Unit, Kirklees Metropolitan Council, 1993).

In Leicester, as part of its 'Environment City' designation, moves are being made to integrate sustainable development criteria into the local economy. The Leicester Environment City Business Forum will provide support for greening the local economy and a 'round table' is being established to analyse priority targets for local policies. Although the scheme is in its early stages, policy options include developing city council purchasing policies and increasing the availability of 'green capital' for developing new business opportunities (Roberts, 1993). Leeds City Council has established the Leeds Environmental Business Forum to offer information on energy, good practice, waste and environmental reviews to small and medium sized firms (Boase and Frank, 1994). Woking Borough Council is addressing the tensions and contradictions between pressures for economic growth and environmental constraints. For example, while enforcement of Green Belt boundaries in Surrey can lead to higher urban densities, it may also lead to the loss of urban open space and green field sites with a resultant decrease in the attractiveness of the local environment and pressures for further decentralisation (Fairlamb, 1993).

Towards an holistic approach

However, an important point which emerges from many current local authority environmental statements and strategies is that few of them are explicitly concerned with industry and employment. In seeking to understand the consequences of developing a sustainable local economy, industry and employment are crucial areas which need to be addressed. At present, environmental strategies and economic development plans are generated from quite different perspectives - a reflection of their historic division and roots. While the former have largely evolved from environmental health departments with their emphasis on protection, the latter have frequently developed from planning functions. From an environmental health perspective, industry is often seen as the *problem* which only crops up in statements in relation to curbing its negative impacts such as air and water pollution or in transport planning. From a planning or local economic development perspective, industry is largely seen as a source of wealth or employment creation. The implication for developing *strong* sustainable development within a local economy is the need to integrate economic development issues with environmental strategies (Gibbs, 1994c).

Understanding the implications of sustainable development at the local level involves envisaging future sustainable scenarios. Four issues are associated with such alternative future scenarios:

- a set of perceptions;
- a response to prevailing trends;
- a body of plans and policies aimed at operationalising the future model in practice; and
- developing new structures to bring the policies to fruition.

In essence, increasing numbers of local authorities already have a perception of the problematic issues through their identification of the traditional concerns of pollution, waste, energy, transport and so on, and have responded by producing audits and environmental statements. However, there is a paucity of plans and policies to redirect the local economy along *strong* sustainability lines, as opposed to those which address *weak* sustainability. To reiterate, what are needed are plans and policies which take an holistic approach to economy environment interrelationships (Gibbs, 1994d).

Existing UK statutory requirements provide the context within which redirection of the local economy can begin to occur. First, the Local Government and Housing Act (1989) requires local authorities to produce an economic development plan, detailing the policies and programmes that an authority intends to introduce over the coming year. This legislation also provides for a process of consultation between the local authority and other bodies in the local community, such as the private sector, the voluntary sector and trade unions. This offers an ideal forum to explore the interrelationship between economic and environmental issues. Second, the policy agenda can be developed through the planning process. The Planning and Compensation Act 1991 and revised guidance on Development Plans could help implement *stronger* forms of sustainable development. Thus, Government advice on planning and the environment recommends:

> that all authorities should carry out an environmental appraisal of every plan as it is produced. The central message is that authorities should take environmental considerations comprehensively, and consistently into account, and integrate environmental concerns into all planning policies. (HM Government, 1992, p.65)

Third, the statutory UK requirement for local authorities to produce Unitary Development Plans (UDPs) and District Development Plans (DDPs) provides a mechanism for local authorities to address the environment and development from a strategic viewpoint (Marshall, 1993). Unitary Development Plans also offer the means for consultation and increased participation. Integrating the economic with the environmental through these instruments also provides a mechanism for implementing Agenda 21, which emphasises the need for dialogue with local organisations, private enterprises and the community. The timescale for this is brief, with the process of consultation and the achievement of consensus on a local Agenda 21 expected by 1996 (UNCED, 1992). Fourth, the UDPs and DDPs are the main reference point for planning decisions, and development is presumed to take place in accordance with the plan, rather than a presumption in favour of development (Bosworth, 1993).

These plans and policies are the means by which sustainable development can be achieved at the local level within the UK. However, it is questionable whether existing local authority organisational structures are adequate for the task of developing sustainable local economies. Historically, the environmental role of UK local authorities stemmed from their provision of core protective services and enforcing base line criteria. Local authorities in time became protective agencies for health and safety, water and air pollution monitoring, food law enforcement and the protection of the physical environment. These functions are predominantly the responsibility of environmental health departments while strategic planning is the province of separate departments, such as planning or economic development. Some consideration needs to be given to the most appropriate structures for the implementation of sustainable development. Should a sustainable development strategy be the responsibility of one department or coordinated between several? Should a separate department be created to implement policy? Should sustainable development be the central guiding principle of all departments rather than hived off into a separate department? These are issues which are currently being addressed through the medium of model management structures and systems (Richards, 1992).

It has been recognised that even implementing *weak* sustainable development policies requires specialised management forms in industry and commerce. To this end, the British Standards Institution Environmental Management Systems standard (BS7750) has been devised and tested, while the EU has recently published its own proposals for *corporate ecological audits*. The Department of the Environment and the Local Government Management Board have investigated the potential application of this Eco-Audit regulation for local authorities, and individual local authorities have investigated adopting BS7750 (Richards, 1992). Such management systems may be essential as environmental policy poses particular problems for local authorities as a consequence of the cross-departmental nature of the issues involved. To achieve successful implementation of a local sustainable development strategy, a fully integrated environmental management system will be needed, with responsibilities at senior management level. While adopting BS7750 or Eco-Audit regulation may not actively promote the strong form of sustainable development, they do provide a mechanism 'to ensure that **whatever** environmental aims a ... council adopts, it tries to act on them, and keeps itself (and in Eco-Audit's case, also the public) well and regularly informed about how well or badly it is succeeding in working towards them' (Levett and Jacobs, 1993, p. 8). What this means is that if sustainable development aims are adopted by local authorities, then having an environmental management system in place is a powerful tool to ensure that they are acted upon.

Conclusions: Towards local sustainable development?

While some progress on *weak* sustainability has been made to date, it is important to realise that few (if any) local authorities have in place a strategy for *strong* sustainable development. Some local authorities have good policy or strategy commitments and some have a number of good individual projects. It is still rare, however, for strategy and projects to be integrated. While the integration of sustainable development policy and action is in its infancy, it is probably true to say that many of the more creative ideas around sustainable development, in the UK at least, are presently coming from local government. This is especially true compared to UK central government policy on sustainable development, which remains paralysed by its commitment to market forces (see HM Government, 1994). Whether UK local government can remain in the forefront of sustainable development initiatives will largely depend on the resources available to them. In a period of increasing financial stringency, anything other than complying with statutory environmental duties is fast becoming a luxury.

Despite this gloomy prognosis, the trend of policy making at the international and EU scales is encouraging. The agreement reached at the Earth Summit on Agenda 21, while forming an agenda for a global sustainability plan rather than a plan itself, places local authorities at the forefront of implementing sustainable development. It sets out a clear timescale for local consultation and agenda setting by local administrations. Similarly, the EU's Fifth Environmental Action Programme places sustainable development and integration of economic and environmental policies at the top of the European agenda in the period until the end of the century. Again, EU policy is clear that local authorities have a specific role to play in implementing the Programme's policy measures. However, the mechanisms for implementing the Action Programme are vague. An additional problem for UK local authorities is that, while the UK central government is a signatory to these international agreements, the level of commitment is ambiguous to say the least. The UK government is keen to pass on an environment role to local government, but shows no sign of giving the resources with which to do this adequately.

While much will depend upon national policy implementation, there are a number of areas where local authorities can act now to prepare the ground for *strong* sustainable development at the local level. Economic development plans, required by the Local Government and Housing Act, can be constructed around the perspective of integrating economic and environmental policies. The planning process also offers local authorities the opportunity to consider whether existing organisational structures are appropriate for the construction and delivery of these new policy areas. The outcome of this process of policy construction can be the identification of programme areas and the resources needed to achieve these. In this way, local authorities can place pressure on central government to provide adequate funding for environmental policy. The presentation of policies and budgets will test the commitment of central government's recent conversion to sustainable development and its endorsement of Agenda 21. An important agenda can be developed around campaigning for adequate resources to implement *strong* sustainable development and to make central government aware that agreeing to Agenda 21 and the Fifth Environmental Action Programme carries responsibilities of implementation. There are opportunities here for developing networks of local authorities, both within the UK and at EU level, facing similar environmental problems to campaign for more resources. For local authorities, the Action Programme in particular offers opportunities effectively to leapfrog the UK Government on environmental policy by devising a policy response to the Programme's objectives. If (or when) the Structural Funds are 'greened', then there will be real opportunities to put this policy into practice. Pressure to implement the Fifth Action Programme has recently come from the European Parliament and the Socialist Group within the parliament has pressed for the implementation of the Programme to replace the single European market as a central Community objective (Collins, 1993).

These are issues for the short to medium term. In the longer term, there are a number of issues that need consideration in understanding the implications for sustainable development within a local economy. First, there are two key issues in the definition of *strong* sustainability that have barely been addressed, economic welfare and equity, while greater attention has been devoted to the task of integrating the economy and the environment. Thus, it is important that one of the key aims of *strong* sustainable development - a commitment to equity - does not get lost in the process of environmental improvement. The poorer and more marginal groups in a local area should be fully involved in setting the agenda. Such groups may have most to fear from a local *strong* sustainable development strategy (the loss of manual jobs in polluting industries, for example), but perhaps they also have the most to gain (for example, not only through an improved environment, but also through the labour intensive nature of job creation in environmental protection).

Second, there is the question of the appropriate spatial scale at which to approach sustainable development. While the nature of the important environmental problems is global in scale, implementing policy at this level is problematic. Conversely, individual urban areas are too small to cope with environmental problems that stretch across administrative boundaries. However, individual local or regional authorities acting in isolation, as with individual firms or countries acting in isolation, will not 'solve' the environmental problems because of their cross-boundary nature. Indeed, this stresses the need for *strong* sustainable development, since *weak* sustainability measures address only the margins of environmental problems, and also in isolation.

The emphasis in this chapter has been upon understanding the implications of sustainable development for the local economy. However, the local economy itself is an area which has been a point of some contention in industrial geography, with considerable debate over whether economic development measures for local economies can be effective in a world dominated by large corporations and subject to economic restructuring processes operating on a global scale (Swyngedouw, 1989; Amin and Malmberg, 1992). A similar debate needs to take place around the appropriate scale for sustainable development. Approaching sustainable development from the purely local level is not enough. What is needed is an interplay between policy 'from above' (for example, Agenda 21 and EU policy) and 'from below' (in the form of local level initiatives, such as local schemes for pollution control). Indeed, a meso scale role has been envisaged by some as providing a new role for regional planning (see for example Breheny, 1993; Roberts and Tilley, 1993; Steiner and Nauser, 1993). In this chapter, the local level response has formed the main focus, perhaps conditioned by a UK perspective where a regional policy dimension is currently largely lacking. More research needs to be undertaken to establish

163

the relevant spatial scales for effective environmental policy implementation.

Looking further ahead, there could be a role for local authorities to act as the primary agents for integrating and coordinating policy initiatives and to provide a leading role in helping to reduce adverse environmental impacts and enhance positive ones. It has been argued that there is a role for local authorities to act as Local Environment Protection Agencies, whereby local authorities not only put their own environmental functions into a strategic framework, but also coordinate the work of other statutory and voluntary agencies in the area (Harman, 1992). Clearly, this would require much greater levels of cooperation than exist at present and a much greater commitment from national government. If this was to be forthcoming, then in future there would be great potential for joint strategy setting to coordinate regional initiatives (by developing new regional authorities) with local authority policy (CAG Consultants, 1993). However, environmental initiatives which stem solely from local authorities, whether they are within individual departments or are coordinated initiatives, are not enough. These are simply essential elements of broader local and regional initiatives designed to enhance environmental quality, working across all sectors, with business, with community groups and with central government departments and to construct an effective new means of governance to deal with these issues. In addition to integrating the environmental with the economic, a central feature of sustainable development is a concern for participation and democratic action. There is scope for initiatives such as Community Forums where local community groups, local businesses and the local authority would meet to establish local agreements on local environmental tolerances and initiatives. Finally, it is essential to note that local authorities need to have not only the will to introduce sustainable development strategies, but also the powers to do so. Ultimately, these have to come from central government if central government is to be serious about implementing sustainable development.

Acknowledgements

David Gibbs would like to acknowledge the financial support of the Economic and Social Research Council's Global Environmental Change Programme (Grant number L320252132) under which this research is being conducted.

References

Amin, A. and Malmberg, A. (1992), 'Competing structural and institutional influences on the geography of production in Europe', *Environment and Planning A,* vol. 24, pp. 401-416.

Bennett, E. (1992), 'European industry and the environment: the developing role of the EC and a strategy for industry', *European Environment,* vol. 2, no. 6, pp. 2-4.

Boase, M. and Frank, J. (1994), 'Green business links - the Leeds Environmental Business Forum, Workshop at Planning Exchange conference 'Valuing the Environment: Making it Work for Local Economic Development', April, Bramhope.

Bosworth, T. (1993), 'Local authorities and sustainable development', *European Environment,* vol. 3, no. 1, pp. 13-17.

Breheny, M. (1993), 'Planning the sustainable city region', *Town and Country Planning,* vol. 62, no. 4, pp. 71-75.

CAG Consultants (1993), *Regional sustainable development and the EC Fifth Environmental Action Programme,* Discussion Paper for Strathclyde Regional Council, CAG Consultants, Glasgow.

Collins, K. (1993), 'Seeking sustainable development', *European Labour Forum,* Winter 93/94, pp. 25-30.

Commission of the European Communities (1990), *Green paper on the Urban Environment,* CEG, Luxembourg.

Commission of the European Communities (1992), *"Towards Sustainability" - A European Community Programme of Policy and Action in Relation in Relation to the Environment and Sustainable Development,* COM 929230, CEC, Brussels.

Department of the Environment (1993), *UK Strategy for Sustainable development: Consultation Paper,* Department of the Environment, London.

Fairlamb, C. (1993), 'Planning and the environment', Paper presented to the conference on Integrating Regional Economic Development and Environmental Management, University of Nottingham, 12-13 July.

Gibbs, D. (1991), 'Greening the local economy', *Local Economy,* vol. 6, no. 3, pp. 224-239.

Gibbs, D. (1993a), *The Green Local Economy,* Centre for Local Economic Strategies, Manchester.

Gibbs, D. (1993b), 'European environmental policy and local economic development', *European Environment,* vol. 3, no. 5, pp. 18-22.

Gibbs, D. (1994a), *The environmental technology industry in the North West,* Report to INWARD, Manchester Metropolitan University.

Gibbs, D. (1994b), 'Towards the sustainable city: greening the local economy', *Town Planning Review,* vol. 65, no 1, pp. 99-109.

Gibbs, D. (1994c), 'Towards the sustainable region? Integrating economic and environmental development at the local level', in S. Hardy and G. Lloyd (eds) *Sustainable Regions?,* Regional Studies Association, London, pp.97-107.

Gibbs, D. (1994d), 'The implications of sustainable development for industry and   employment in the 1990s', *The Environmentalist,* vol. 14, no.3, pp. 183-192.

Gibbs, D.C. and Healey, M.J. (1994), 'Industrial geography and the environment: understanding sustainable local economies', paper presented to International Geographical Union Commission Conference on the Organisation of Industrial Space Conference on Industry and Environmental Challenge, August 2-6, Budapest, Hungary.

Harman, J. (1992), *The Focal Role of Local Authorities in Environmental Policy,* Kirklees Metropolitan Borough Council, Huddersfield.

HM Government (1992), *The Common Inheritance: The Second Year Report,* Cm2068, HMSO, London.

HM Government (1994), *Sustainable Development,* Justice Kingsley/Regional Studies Association, London.

Haughton, G. and Hunter, C. (1994), *Sustainable Cities,* Justice Kingsley/Regional Studies Association, London.

Hams, T., Jacobs, M., Levett, R., Lusser, H., Morphet, J. and Taylor, D. (1994), *Greening Your Local Authority,* Longman, Harlow.

International Council for Local Environmental Initiatives (1994), *Local Agenda 21 Network News,* 1, June.

Jacobs, M. (1991), *The Green Economy,* Pluto Press, London.

Jacobs, M. (1993), 'A green route out of recession', *New Ground,* vol. 34, pp. 4-5.

Jacobs, M. and Stott, M. (1992), 'Sustainable development and the local economy', *Local Economy,* vol. 7, no. 3, pp. 261-272.

Levett, R. and Jacobs, M. (1993), *Environmental Management Systems and Sustainable Development,* CAG Consultants, London.

Local Government Management Board (1992), *A Statement on behalf of UK Local Government,* LGMB, Luton.

Marshall, T. (1993), 'Sustainable Boroughs?', *Town and Country Planning,* vol. 62, no. 4, pp. 87-89.

Organisation for Economic Cooperation and Development (1990), *Urban Environmental Policies for the 1990s,* OECD, Paris.

Richards, L. (1992), 'Local authority environmental audits: implementation and management systems', *European Environment,* vol. 2, no. 6, pp.16-19.

Roberts, P. and Tilley, F. (1993), 'Sustainable regional economic development and planning', Paper presented to the conference on Integrating Regional Economic Development and Environmental Management, University of Nottingham, 12-13 July.

Roberts, I. (1993), 'Greening the local economy: why and how', Paper presented to the conference on Integrating Regional economic Development and Environmental Management, University of Nottingham, 12-13 July.

Steiner, D. and Nauser, M. (1993), *Human Ecology: Fragments of Anti-Fragmentary Views of the World,* Routledge, London

Street, P. (1992), 'Local authority environmental audits: key factors for success', *European Environment,* vol. 2, no. 6, pp. 20-22.

Stott, M. (1993), 'Economic development and sustainability', paper presented to the conference on Integrating Regional Economic Development and Environmental management, University of Nottingham, 12-13 July.

Swyngedouw, E.A. (1989), 'The heart of the place: the resurrection of locality in an age of hyperspace', *Geografiska Annaler,* Series B, 71B, No. 1, pp. 131-42.

United Nations Conference on Environment and Development (1987), *Our Common Future*, Oxford University Press, Oxford.

9 The role of industrial estates in the creation and destruction of local environments: An Indian experience

M. B. Singh, R. K. Pandey and V. Singh

Introduction

Industrial estates have been created in India to act as growth poles in less developed regions to initiate broad scale social and economic development. In addition they have been set up to make suitable land available to prospective entrepreneurs. However, policy is not only aimed at creating a climate conducive to economic development in these industrial estates, it also provides the opportunity to control and curb atmospheric and other forms of pollution in a regulated manner.

Against this background, this chapter examines and assesses the economic and environmental impacts of the Ram Nagar Industrial Estate in Uttar Pradesh; specifically how this estate stimulates entrepreneurial activity, socio-economic development (especially the creation of employment opportunities) and the impact on and destruction of the local environment through pollution and the discharge of solid and liquid wastes from small and medium scale industries. The estate is three kilometres from Ram Nagar and six kilometres from Varanasi City (Figure 9.1).

To collect data on the structure of industry, the characteristics of entrepreneurs and the nature of pollution in the Ram Nagar industrial estate, a questionnaire survey was undertaken between December 1993 and January 1994 augmented by interviews with workers and managers. This information was combined with data from earlier work by Singh and Singh (1984). In the context of this research, the role of the industrial estate in the creation of a local economic environment has been assessed in terms of changes in entrepreneurial behaviour, the market it provides for local raw materials, the level of demand for manufactured goods in the surrounding area, the

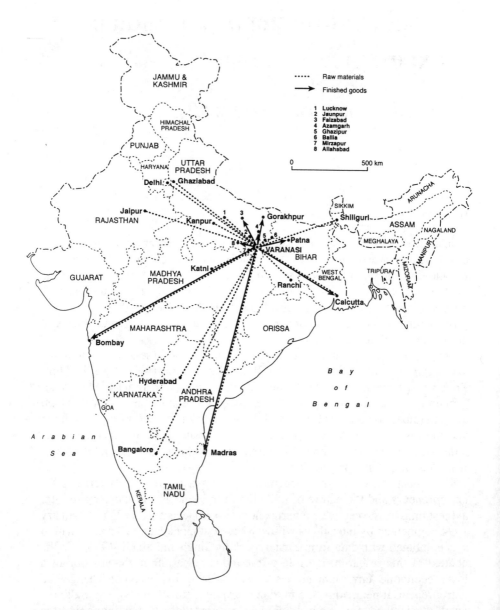

Figure 9.1 The location of the Ram Nagar Industrial Estate and its input output relationships

generation of employment opportunities, and the general socio-economic conditions of local inhabitants. The destruction and damage of the local physical environment has been assessed by collating information on the levels and effects of pollution (noise, water and air), and the discharge of solid and liquid wastes by industry.

An industrial estate can be described as a carefully selected and developed tract of land on which ready-made general purpose factories and certain common facilities and services are provided (Bharti, 1978, p. 10). Bredo (1960) has described an industrial estate as a tract of land which is subdivided and developed according to a comprehensive plan for use by a community of advanced industrial enterprises. According to Alexander (1963), an industrial estate may be defined as 'a group of factories constructed on an economic scale in suitable sites with facilities of water, transport, electricity, steam, bank, post offices, canteen, watch and ward and first aid, and provided with special arrangements for technical guidance and common service facilities' (Alexander, 1963, p. 5).

Initially the creation of industrial estates in India was to promote the planned growth of 'small scale' industries. During the period of the Second Five Year Plan (1956-1960), the Small-Scale Industries Board of the Government of India instigated the creation of 14 industrial estates in the State of Uttar Pradesh. The strategy was modified somewhat during the period of the Third Five Year Plan (1961-1965), with greater emphasis being placed on the establishment of industrial estates in small towns and rural areas. As a result, 53 new industrial estates were created during this period, a process that continued through the Fifth Five Year Plan (1974-1978) and beyond. Industrial estates were seen as a basic tool for the development of 'backward' areas, or areas with no industrial presence. Currently, there are 110 industrial estates established in Uttar Pradesh.

In 1988, the Government of India instigated a scheme to develop growth centres in all states and union territories to promote industrialisation in 'backward' areas (Government of India, 1988, p. 107). These new growth centres were to be provided with adequate infrastructure, such as power, water, and communications, so they could act as magnets to attract industry to these areas. A total of 70 growth centres are to be developed during the period of the Eighth Plan (1992-1997), of which six centres are to be established in Uttar Pradesh.

Environmental legislation and pollution control

At present, there are more than 200 Central and State laws in India which either directly or indirectly serve to protect the environment. The major pieces of legislation affecting environmental protection are: The Wildlife

171

(Protection) Act, 1972; The Water (Prevention and Control of Pollution) Act, 1974 (amended in 1978); The Water Cess Act, 1977, amended in 1987 as the Water (Prevention and Control of Pollution) Cess Act; The Air (Prevention and Control of Pollution) Act, 1981, amended in 1987; The Environment (Protection) Act, 1986; The National Forest Policy, 1988; and the Draft Policy Statement for Abatement of Pollution, 1991. Arguably the most important development in recent years has been the adoption of The National Conservation Strategy and Policy Statement on Environment and Development, adopted by the Indian Government in June 1992. 'The policy document has enlisted the specific requirements for environmental orientation needed for sustainable development in some key sectors - agriculture, irrigation, animal husbandry, forestry, energy, transportation and human settlements' (Nijhawan, 1993).

Legislative Acts, including The Environment (Protection) Act of May 1986, are clearly targeted specifically towards conservation, whereas pre 1972 legislation always had other primary objectives. Nijhawan (1993) argues that the new priority given in India to environmental concerns can be attributed to a UN sponsored meeting on the environment in Stockholm in 1972. The Environment (Protection) Act of May 1986 is arguably a powerful weapon in the hands of Government to improve the quality of the environment and for controlling and indeed abating polluting activities. For example, there is no specific legislation in force in India concerning noise pollution, there are only unco-ordinated provisions within other legislative instruments. Singh and Bains (1987) have examined the issue of environmental noise pollution, and have argued that there is an urgent need to enact some form of comprehensive legislation for the control of noise pollution in India.

As enacted, environmental legislation has provided for the establishment of Air Pollution and Water Pollution Control Boards at a national and state level. These boards have the power to both issue and revoke licences for polluting industries, to impose and enforce emission standards, and to frame rules and regulations to control water and air pollution. Heavily polluted areas may be declared 'air pollution control areas' by a State Government following consultation with the State Boards, where further pollution through the use of certain fuels would become a health hazard to local residents and workers. No industrial plant can be operated in an 'air pollution control area' by any company or individual without the consent of the State Board. In a recent case, the Apex Court of India ordered the immediate closure of 190 industrial units located on the banks of the river Ganga due to their failure to install appropriate pollution control devices (Nijhawan, 1993).

Various penalties can be imposed upon those who contravene environmental legislation: The Water Act allows for the imposition of a Rs. 5000 (approximately US $160) fine, and/or imprisonment of up to six years; the Air Act limits maximum imprisonment to three months and a fine of Rs.

5000. Following the enactment of the new Environmental (Protection) Act of 1986, the term of imprisonment can be up to seven years, and/or a fine of up to Rs. 100,000 (approximately US $3,200).

The industrial structure of the Ram Nagar Industrial Estate

The Ram Nagar Industrial Estate currently contains a variety of small and medium sized enterprises involved in such activities as paper and paper board manufacture, dairy production, cattle feed production, cement pipe manufacture, textiles, metal utensils, chemicals and engineering. Only two of the enterprises located on the industrial estate could be described as large concerns and 23 per cent of enterprises have been established since 1990.

Approximately 50 per cent of enterprises on the industrial estate are concerned with either chemicals or animal and forest based products. The average size of each enterprise, in terms of employment is 25 and enterprises engaged in agriculture and forest based activities tend to employ the largest numbers of workers (Table 9.1). Significantly, the growth and development of service industries in the industrial estate is increasing employment opportunities.

Almost 70 per cent of all businesses on the industrial estate provide employment to only 20 persons, 35 per cent do not even legally qualify as a factory as they employ less than 10 persons, and only 5 per cent of enterprises employ more than 40 workers. In terms of productive capital (input and output) nearly all enterprises can be classified as small since nearly 70 per cent of them have input and output levels between Rs. 1 (approximately US $0.03) and Rs. 1 million (approximately US $32,000).

The creation of a local economic environment

Changes in the local economic environment associated with the creation of the Ram Nagar Industrial Estate can be identified in changes in entrepreneurial behaviour. Markets for local raw materials have changed, local market areas for manufactured products have changed, employment opportunities have been created and there has been a general socio-economic 'uplift' - all of which, it can be argued, are attributable to the establishment of the industrial estate. Four major changes in the local economic environment can be attributed to the establishment of the industrial estate.

First, local entrepreneurship has been enhanced. Indeed, 94 per cent of the entrepreneurs in the industrial estate are 'local'. An unpublished survey of the area conducted in 1985 by Papola and Tewari revealed a far lower percentage of local participation, and recent improvements have been attributed to government incentives and encouragement to local entrepreneurs.

173

Various schemes to encourage young entrepreneurs have been instigated, such as the self-employment scheme. As a result of this government encouragement, the average age of the entrepreneurs in the industrial estate is 40. Approximately 12 per cent of the entrepreneurs are aged 30 or less, whilst 53 per cent fall into the 30-40 year age range. All categories of industry in the industrial estate exhibit this same youthful age profile.

The estate's entrepreneurs are predominantly graduates with first and higher degrees (Table 9.2). Only 6 per cent have less than degree standard education, and these less qualified entrepreneurs tend to be concentrated in the forest and metal products sectors.

Table 9.1
Industrial structure of Ram Nagar industrial estate

Type of Industry	No. of units	Employment				Input (lakh Rs.)			Output (lakh Rs.)		
		<10	10-20	20-40	>40	1-5	5-10	>10	1-5	5-10	>10
Animal forest based	9	3	2	2	2	2	5	1	2	4	2
Chemical products	9	4	3	2	-	3	1	5	3	-	6
Metal products	4	1	2	1	-	1	1	2	1	1	2
Ceramics	4	2	2	-	-	2	2	-	2	2	-
Textile products	5	1	1	3	-	3	1	1	2	2	1
Engineering	4	2	2	-	-	1	2	1	1	1	2

Source: Survey by the authors

Notwithstanding their educational qualifications most entrepreneurs in the Ram Nagar Industrial Estate have come from industrial backgrounds (53 per cent). Only 18 per cent have started their present ventures under the self-employed scheme immediately on completion of their studies.

The contribution of the 'non-business' community to the establishment of new industrial enterprises in the Ram Nagar Industrial Estate is, at 44 per cent, very substantial, illustrating a healthy trend in the changing entrepreneurial environment of the country. Brahmins (formerly engaged in religious and educational employment) and Rajput (associated with the military) have contributed significantly to this change (Table 9.3). It appears that the overall development of the industrial estate has encouraged the entry of a large number of entrepreneurs into industrial activity, who have not previously been involved in industry as a family or caste occupation.

Second, the jobs generated in the industrial estate have predominantly been taken up by locals. Indeed, 55 per cent of workers reside in the local area and 82 per cent of employees reside within the Varanasi district. In terms of skills, 42 per cent of the estate's workers are unskilled, 32 are semi-skilled and 27 per cent are described as skilled. However, of the small proportion of workers from outside the State of Uttar Pradesh, the majority are skilled, suggesting the beginnings of a possible skills deficit in the region (Table 9.4).

Workers from outside Uttar Pradesh make up a considerable share of total employment in the dairy, engineering and chemicals industries. This take up of jobs in the Ram Nagar Industrial estate by local people is a commonpattern in industrial estates elsewhere in India. The only exceptions occur where technical training institutes have been established within a locality.

Third, the Ram Nagar Industrial Estate has fostered distinctive patterns of local raw materials usage and strong local sales. Raw materials consumed by the animal and forest based products sector are locally sourced from within the State, whereas the chemical, engineering, textile, metal work and cement industries tend to source materials from outside the immediate local area. Approximately 50 per cent of raw materials for cattle feed enterprises (e.g., ground nuts, linseed, mustard cake, rice polish and grains) are directly sourced from Maharashtra. Caustic soda, LDPE (a type of plastic), sulphate chemical cotton, DOP, sodium chloride, dies, iron plate, silica powder, cast iron, steel rods, bauxite, fire clay and steromac (thermocoal) are obtained from Madras, Bangalore, Hyderabad, Bombay, Calcutta, Jaipur, Delhi and Bihar State. The Kanpur industrial hub supplies approximately 75 per cent of the raw materials sourced from within Uttar Pradesh. Only 18 per cent of the estate's industrial units consume or utilise local raw materials (Table 9.5)

Of the finished products from enterprises in the Ram Nagar Industrial Estate, approximately 85 per cent are sold within the State of Uttar Pradesh, particularly to customers in nearby localities such as Varanasi, Azamgargh, Allahabad, Gorakhpur, Faizabad, Ghazipur, Janupur, Ballia and Mirzapur districts (Figure 9.1). Only electric fans manufactured on the industrial estate are sold outside Uttar Pradesh.

Fourth, the setting up of the Ram Nagar Industrial Estate has led to significant infrastructure development. Following the establishment of the estate, subsidiary activities such as transport and communications, shopping, banking facilities, repair and domestic services have increased. Whilst only in isolated pockets and in small numbers, these activities represent embryonic external economic benefits to the local economy. The meagreness of this development of ancillary services is, in part, due to the paucity of funds to

175

Table 9.2
Characteristics of Entrepreneurs

Type of Industry	Age in years				Qualification			Previous Activity				
	<30	30-40	40-50	>50	Inter	Graduate	Master & higher	Industry	Trade	Service	Profes-sional	Self-employed
Animal & forest based	-	5	2	1	1	6	1	5	2	1	-	-
Chemical products	1	5	3	-	-	8	1	5	3	-	-	1
Metal Products	1	2	-	1	1	2	1	2	1	-	-	1
Ceramics	-	2	1	1	-	3	1	1	-	-	1	2
Textile products	1	2	2	-	-	2	3	4	1	-	-	-
Engineering	1	2	-	1	-	2	2	1	-	-	1	2
Total	4	18	8	4	2	23	9	18	7	1	2	6

Source: Survey by the authors

Table 9.3
Community contribution to ownership

Community	Percentage
Business	56
Non-Business	44
(i) Brahmin	33
(ii) Rajput	27
(iii) Srivastava	13
(iv) Others	27

Source: Survey by the authors

Table 9.4
Share of employment by region of origin

Worker category	Total (%)	Originating outside Uttar Pradesh	From within Uttar Pradesh	From within Varanasi district	Originiating within 10km
Unskilled	41	>1	2	11	29
Semi-skilled	32	1	8	11	12
Skilled	27	4	3	6	14

Source: Survey by the authors

both create and augment sufficient infrastructure. Interaction between politicians, government officers and contractors has further worsened the situation through the extraction of 'commissions' from monies allocated for infrastructure development. This is of course not unique to Ram Nagar or Uttar Pradesh, it is a situation prevalent throughout India (Behari, 1994, pp. 41-43). Approximately 85 per cent of entrepreneurs express a deep concern over the problems of water and electricity supply. It would appear that many plots on the industrial estate lie vacant due to the paucity of service provision.

Table 9.5
Sources of raw materials

Category	Locally sourced	Within Uttar Pradesh	Uttar Pradesh and outside	Outside Uttar Pradesh
Animal & forest based	6	1	-	1
Chemical	-	-	4	5
Metal	-	2	-	2
Ceramic	-	-	2	2
Textile	-	-	1	4
Engineering	-	-	2	2

Source: Survey by the authors

Destruction of the local environment: air pollution, water pollution, noise and solid wastes

Atmospheric pollution became an issue with the Indian Government and the population in general in the aftermath of the Bhopal gas tragedy in 1984 when 3,300 people lost their lives. A leak of highly toxic MIC from the Union Carbide plant dispersed quickly into the surrounding area, making Bhopal the world's second biggest atmospheric pollution episode after the London Smog of 1952 (4,000 deaths). The tragedy focused governmental and public attention on the potential dangers of atmospheric pollution, both gaseous and particulate. Emissions of carbon dioxide, carbon monoxide, oxides of nitrogen, hydrocarbons and sulphur dioxide are potential gaseous pollution problems. Particulate pollutants, such as asbestos, aerosols, mercury, and lead, are also problematic. In the case of the Ram Nagar Industrial Estate the main source of pollution is the use of coal, diesel and petrol as fuel. In combination, some 32 per cent of the estate's industrial units consume 3,893 tonnes of coal per annum, emitting large quantities of dust and gaseous pollutants. The use of diesel to fuel emergency generators, and the burning of refuse, also add to the pollution in the industrial estate (Table 9.6).

Water pollution is a problem specific to a number of enterprises in the Ram Nagar Industrial Estate. Approximately 9,255 litres (3.37 million litres per annum) are consumed on a daily basis by dairy, paper, pharmaceutical, smokeless coal and PVC pipe manufacturing enterprises in the industrial

178

estate (29 per cent of enterprises). The paper, dairy and pharmaceutical firms also discharge a large amount of waste water. On average, the paper

Table 9.6
Estimated emissions of gaseous pollutants (kg per annum)

Sources	Nitrogen oxide	Sulphur dioxide	Carbon Monoxide	Hydrocarbon as methane
Coal	35,311	134,180	5,297	1,766
Diesel	277	673	235	740

Source: Survey by the authors

industry alone discharges between 189,250 and 378,500 litres of waste water per tonne of paper manufactured (Kumra, 1982, p.42). Pollutants discharged by the paper and dairy industries, which include chemical and biological contaminants (e.g., sulphur, nitrogenous wastes and bacteria) can enter the ground water and pollute domestic water sources in the surrounding area. There is no provision for the safe disposal of water used in industrial processes. Proper sewerage facilities are completely absent. Groundwater contamination, especially by the paper industry, could prove to be particularly problematic (Pawar, 1987). To examine the extent of groundwater pollution in the vicinity of the estate, water samples from five wells were collected and analysed. The results are reported in Table 9.7.

Although the analyses indicate that well water in the vicinity of the industrial estate is suitable for irrigation, samples 2 and 3 show as being unsuitable for drinking, and are located close to the industrial estate. Whilst the situation with regard to groundwater contamination is not at present grave, further development of the industrial estate could potentially prove disastrous for local water supplies. It would seem prudent at this stage in the development of the industrial estate to construct proper sewerage treatment facilities to prevent future groundwater contamination. After adequate processing, the liquid wastes could be used for irrigation, provided adequate treatment was made available, such as oxidation ponds, anaerobic treatment or short detention ponds, all of which are well suited to the situation in India (Arveivala, 1993, p. 48). Anaerobic treatment, during which 80 per cent of water purification takes place, is ideal for India's tropical climate. The near zero power requirement for this process makes it a particularly suitable and sustainable process for water treatment. However, there is also a need for

Table 9.7
Assessment of the effect of waste water disposal on groundwater pollution

Sample Well No.	Hardness (ppm)		pH		Sulphate (ppm)		Nitrate (ppm)	
	existing	permissible	existing	permissible	existing	permissible	existing	permissible
1	180	200	7.6	7-8.5	52	200	18	20
2	210	200	8.4	7-8.5	88	200	23	20
3	212	200	8.1	7-8.5	92	200	24	20
4	150	200	7.8	7-8.5	63	200	18	20
5	165	200	7.5	7-8.5	47	200	19	20

Source: Survey by the authors

some degree of post anaerobic treatment to reduce the levels of pollutants in liquid wastes and to meet effluent control standards. A process of simple aeration could quite easily take care of this final processing stage.

Noise pollution from the Ram Nagar Industrial Estate is not a particularly major problem since the estate is located some distance from the main residential and city areas, and it also contains only units of small or medium size. The ambient noise level within the industrial estate varies between 50 to 60 dB, well within the prescribed limit of 75 dB for industrial areas. While noise does not present itself as a problem in the area, it would seem prudent to encourage public awareness of the potential harmful effects of noise pollution, and to encourage the formulation of more specific noise control legislation.

The disposal of solid wastes is a world wide problem, not one confined to the Ram Nagar Industrial Estate. Some 240 tonnes of various solid wastes, comprising iron, aluminium, rubber, broken ampoules and other more organic refuse, are disposed of each year from the industrial estate. The form of refuse generated from the industrial estate is mostly unsuitable for composting and, therefore, needs to be properly collected and disposed of in landfill sites.

The perception of industrial pollution

To examine their perceptions of pollution, entrepreneurs on the industrial estate were asked about the pollution generated by their enterprises, the effects on workers and any measures taken to prevent or reduce levels of pollution. It appears that all were well aware of the problems posed by pollution. Nevertheless, 90 per cent seemed indifferent to pollution control measures. The main attempt at pollution control was through the erection of chimneys, and 35 per cent of entrepreneurs had constructed chimneys to 'reduce' pollution. However only 8 per cent had constructed chimneys over 50 feet in height. Below this level chimneys offer less local pollution control. Many respondents who favoured pollution control blamed poor advice and even the complete absence of advice from government officials.

It would appear that environmental legislation, particularly with regard to pollution control, has not been implemented for a range of reasons including:

- the current lack of training for local government officials in pollution control;
- the insufficient training of the staff of Central and State Pollution Boards to implement pollution control legislation;
- the consistent underfunding of Central and State Pollution Boards;
- the poor standard of environmental education in general, with the general public having little or no knowledge of potential environmental hazards. Environmental legislation is of little or no importance without public understanding;
- the requirement for only new enterprises to have pollution certification, with older ones having to be persuaded to adopt pollution control measures.

A wide range of measures could be adopted to address the paucity of environmental regulation, and consequent environmental degradation. These would enhance environmental conditions in all India's industrial estates, including the one at Ram Nagar. First, more research and development is required on more reliable and non-polluting alternative energy sources. Limitations of power supplies have proved problematic to entrepreneurs. Factory owners need to install on-site gravity settling chambers, fabric filters, effluent treatment facilities and so on, to cut down on pollution discharges. Indeed, larger firms need to employ pollution control specialists to monitor the efficacy of pollution control. The enforcement of environmental standards needs to be uniform. Many small firms have established themselves on the estate but compete with larger firms by spending less on pollution controls and maintenance of environmental standards. Loans for the expansion of businesses should only be granted if enterprises adopt necessary pollution control measures, and noise pollution legislation needs to be enacted before the problem becomes critical.

Environmental management should be free from political interference and corruption to allow impartial implementation of environmental laws. Environmental information needs to be disseminated throughout India. Proper and professional training on environmental issues should be implemented for all administrators, and pollution boards must be supplied with adequate equipment to monitor pollution. Indeed, it would seem appropriate for the Indian Government to produce an annual 'State of the Environment Report' for the country as a whole.

Conclusions

The Ram Nagar Industrial Estate has played a significant role in changing the local economic environment, promoting entrepreneurial behaviour, and providing employment opportunities and products for local consumption. The government's self-employment schemes could be used to further expand the creation of businesses, especially in the agribusiness sector.

Growing concern within India over the problems posed by increasing levels of environmental degradation has resulted in some positive action. Environmental awareness campaigns have been instigated at the behest of the government to promote understanding of the problems associated with pollution and methods of afforestation and eco-regeneration. There has also been an acceptance of the fact that 'it is the poor who bear the brunt of ecological degradation, while the fruits of development planning and progress are usurped by the affluent sections of Society' (Nijhawan, 1993). Nijhawan has also argued that there is a 'grass roots' element to the current improvement in environmental understanding. Those directly affected by environmental degradation are 'now asserting their right of survival and are questioning the old paradigm of development' (Nijhawan, 1993).

Environmental degradation due to pollution is currently quite minor in and around the Ram Nagar Industrial Estate. However, further growth and development could create a great many new environmental problems, especially from the use of coal and diesel as sources of energy and from the disposal of solid and liquid wastes. Current legislation may well be ineffective in the future if current standards of enforcement and monitoring are allowed to continue.

References

Alexander, P.C. (1963), *Industrial Estates in India,* Asia Publishing House, Bombay.

Arceivala, S.J. (1993), 'Simple Systems Available to Treat Sewage', *Down to Earth,* April 15, p. 48.

Behari, M. (1994), 'Where to invest in a country of extremes', *Asia Money,* April, pp. 41-43.

Bharti, M. (1978), *Industrial Estates in Developing Economies,* National, New Delhi.

Bredo, W. (1960), *Industrial Estates: Tool for Industrialisation,* International Industrial Development Centre, Stanford Research Institute, USA.

Government of India (1988), *Eighth Five Year Plan (1992-1997),* Government of India Planning Commission, New Delhi.

Kumra, V.K. (1982), *Kanpur City: A Study in environmental Pollution,* Tara Book Agency, Varanasi.

Nijhawan, N.R. (1993), *Global Environmental Change: India's Response and Initiatives,* Indian Council of Social Science Research, New Delhi.

Papola, T.S and Tewari, R.T. (1985), *Industrial Development of Backward Areas,* Satvahan Publications, New Delhi.

Pawar, N.J. et al. (1987), 'Impact of Human Activities on the Quality of Water in the Mutha Right Bank Canal, Pune City Area', *Transactions of the Institute of Indian Geographers* vol. 9, no. 2, pp. 25-33.

Singh, G.P. and Bains, M.S. (1987), 'Management of Noise Pollution', In Sapru, R.K. (ed) *Environment Management in India: Volume II,* Ashish Publishing House, New Delhi.

Singh, M.B. and Singh, A.K. (1984), 'Impact of Ram Nagar Industrial Area on Local Environs - A Survey', *Rural Systems* vol. VIJ, no. 4, pp. 41-48.

Index

destruction 22-23, 28, 32, 49, 60, 85, 124, 130, 169, 171, 178
deterritorialisation 13, 28
detoxification 86
dialectics 11, 35, 53, 78
disempowerment 43, 71-73
eco-balance 92, 97
eco-balances 84, 92, 97, 103
eco-system 25
ecocentric 4, 5, 18-20, 24, 31, 58
ecocentrism 18
ecosystem 21, 25, 31, 90, 133
embeddedness 9, 14, 68, 69, 78
empowerment 34, 43, 71-73
ESCAP 132, 149, 150
exploitation 3-4, 8-9, 32, 38, 69, 87
flexibility 41, 53
Fordism 37-40, 42-43, 54, 81
foreign-owned 138
France 78, 104, 114
Frankfurt 125
Gaia 19, 20, 31, 34
gatekeepers 120-122
Germany 66, 79, 100, 112, 113, 115, 120, 121, 123
Glasgow 165
global 7, 11-13, 18, 25, 27-30, 37, 39, 41, 48, 50, 53, 57-59, 61, 63, 64, 76-80, 85, 86, 90, 91, 102, 115, 125, 157, 161-164, 183
government 8-10, 59, 67, 73, 87, 110-115, 121-123, 126-127, 129, 132-133, 135-136, 141, 144-147, 149, 151-155, 157, 159-164, 166, 171-174, 177-178, 181-183
Greenpeace 87, 105
hazards 11, 181
hierarchy 25
Hydro-Quebec 108, 110-114, 121, 122, 125, 126

India 127, 169, 171, 172, 175, 177, 179, 181-183
Indonesia 130-132, 148
industrial districts 20, 29, 32, 40, 160, 166
industry 7, 9, 14, 41, 52, 62, 66, 77, 78, 81, 85-88, 90, 92, 98-101, 104, 105, 123, 125, 131, 136, 137, 139, 150, 156-160, 165, 166, 169, 171, 174, 175, 179
infrastructure 107, 122, 134, 136, 140, 144, 153, 171, 175, 177
innovation 33, 73, 79, 99, 101, 158
inventories 42, 44, 92
investment 14, 43, 58, 66, 70, 75, 76, 91, 100, 101, 138, 141, 157
Ireland 124, 155
isomorphism 73
jobs 37, 40, 42-45, 60, 91, 153, 157, 162, 175
just-in-time 41, 42, 44, 54
Karlsruhe 124
keiretsu 80
Kirklees 158, 166
Korea 129, 130, 133, 136, 149
labour 1, 8, 13, 37, 39-45, 50, 53, 54, 58, 60, 61, 64, 66, 69, 70, 73, 79, 80, 131, 136, 137, 139, 162, 165
landscape 3, 4, 54, 57, 60, 104, 124, 150
legislation 88, 101, 104, 131, 141, 144, 145, 153, 154, 159, 171, 172, 180-182
Leicester 158
local/global 30
locality 40, 41, 60, 61, 64, 73, 77, 167, 175
Malaysia 130, 131, 133, 148, 150

186